*The French Revolution
and the Church*

The French Revolution and the Church

JOHN MCMANNERS

HARPER TORCHBOOKS
Harper & Row, Publishers
New York and Evanston

THE FRENCH REVOLUTION AND THE CHURCH

Copyright © 1969 by John McManners.

Printed in the United States of America.

This book was originally published by S. P. C. K., London, in 1969.
It is here reprinted by arrangement.

First HARPER TORCHBOOK edition published 1970 by
Harper & Row, Publishers, Inc.
49 East 33rd St.
New York, New York 10016

Contents

In the year's sabbatical leave from the University of Sydney during which (together with more detailed researches on another theme) the reading for this book was completed, I enjoyed the generous hospitality and friendship of the Warden and Fellows of All Souls College. This small volume, the preliminary instalment of the harvest of that delightful year, gives me my first opportunity to express my gratitude.

John McManners

University of Leicester.

Time Chart, 1789-1795

1789

4 May	Procession and Mass for opening of Estates General
13 June	Three *curés* join the commons
17 June	"National Assembly"
19 June	Vote of the clergy to join the "General Assembly"
20 June	Tennis Court Oath
23 June	Séance royale
14 July	Fall of the Bastille
4 August	"Night of the 4th August"—renunciation of privileges
11 August	The clergy finally abandon tithe
5 October	March of the women to Versailles
2 November	Church property "at the disposal of the nation"
4 November	M. J. Chénier's *Charles IX* staged

1790

5 February	The Assembly adds new members to its Ecclesiastical Committee
13 February	Treilhard's decree on monasticism
12 April	Dom Gerle's motion

1792

15 April	The Festival of Liberty (Fête de Châteauvieux)
20 April	Declaration of war on Austria
26 May	New decree against refractory priests (vetoed)
20 June	Mob invade the Tuileries
10 August	Fall of the Throne
14 August	Further decree against the clergy
2 September	Prison massacres
20 September	French victory at Valmy. *État civil* laicized and divorce legalized
19 November	Decree—France will help other peoples to liberty
20 December	Trial of the King

1793

21 January	Execution of the King
1 February	Declaration of war on England and Holland
7 March	Declaration of war on Spain
10 March	Revolt in the Vendée
18 March	Battle of Neerwinden
6 April	Committee of Public Safety
2 June	Expulsion of Girondins
4 June	Creation of *Armée révolutionnaire*
13 July	Murder of Marat
10 August	Fête for the new Constitution
23 August	*Levée en masse*
22 September	"Feast of Brutus" at Nevers (Fouché)
1 October	De-Christianization at Abbeville

7 October	Revolutionary Calendar adopted (Vendémiaire 16, An II)
15 October	Trial of Girondins
16 October	Execution of the Queen
10 November	Fête of Reason in Notre-Dame (Brumaire 20; An II)

1794

23 March	Execution of Hébertistes (Germinal 3; An II)
5 April	Execution of Dantonists
7 May	Culte de l'Être Suprême (Floréal 18; An II)
8 June	Fête de l'Être Suprême (Prairial 20; An II)
28 July	Execution of Robespierre (Thermidor 10; An II)
12 November	Jacobin Club closed

1795

21 February	Decree of Boissy d'Anglas (separation of Church and State)
30 May	Declaration of Submission to laws of the Republic
September	New oath on the clergy
26 October	The Directory

1. *The Crisis of 1788*

In November 1788 the story was current that Malesherbes, Louis XVI's reforming minister, had advised his sovereign to read Hume on the fate of Charles I of England. "Your position, Sire, is the same as his: the issue is joined between the royal power, as it has been exercised in the past, and the demands of the citizens. Fortunately", he added, distinguishing the approaching crisis in France from the English Civil War of the seventeenth century, "religious quarrels are not involved". "Ah", replied the King, seizing on the optimistic side of the argument, "that's right; it's most fortunate, for there won't be the same bitterness—*l'atrocité ne sera pas la même*". As to the outcome, they were mistaken and the bitterness was greater than anyone could have imagined. But was Malesherbes right as regards the essence of the situation in 1788? Were religious issues inevitably involved in the approaching Revolution, or did they become entangled in the revolutionary events through a series of tragic, avoidable actions?

Up to the end of 1788 Malesherbe's analysis fitted the facts: the central theme of events in France was a struggle against royal "despotism". The attack was led by the aristocracy, buzzing like gilded hornets at the proposals of Louis' Controller-General, Calonne, to end their exemptions from taxation, part of his plan to save the state from bankruptcy. It was a complex revolt by the members of a richly diversified class, in part defending privilege, in part manoeuvring for the right of leadership, nationally and locally, now that the absolutism was faltering. In this war between the Crown and an incoherent uprising of *grands seigneurs* and country squires,

1

magistrates of Parlements and intriguing courtiers, the aristocratic prelates of France played their parts. On the King's
side was Loménie de Brienne, Archbishop of Toulouse, who
took over as first minister when Calonne fell from power in
May 1787–a luxurious unbeliever who called on his countrymen for financial sacrifices, and awarded himself huge compensations in promotions and benefices when he left office a
few months later. This archbishop, who spent more time
leaning on his billiard cue than in saying masses, typified the
foundering *ancien régime,* both in his vices and in his specious
flair for administrative manipulation. As a churchman he had
risen to high responsibilities solely because of noble birth;
intellectually he belonged to the party of the *philosophes*; in
politics it was his ambition to be a great cardinal statesman in
the succession of Richelieu and Mazarin, Dubois and Fleury.
Like them, indeed, he obtained a cardinal's hat, but his rule
was quickly overturned, thanks largely to the opposition of
his ecclesiastical colleagues who, in defying his policies, gave
decisive formulation to the more idealistic aspirations of the
revolt of the aristocracy.

One reason why Brienne had been given charge of the affairs
of the Crown was the hope that the Clergy (that is, the aristocratic churchmen who sat in the Assembly General of the
clergy of France) would vote generous subsidies at the request
of an archbishop. But his application was treated with contempt. He asked eight million livres and the Assembly voted
1,800,000. The remonstrance of the Clergy to the King on
15 June 1788 explained their action in words that lifted the
aristocratic revolt onto a new plane of dignity and universality.
Alone in the nation the clergy had retained the right to vote
taxes freely. Their insistence on this privilege was not a selfish
determination to retain a "particular exemption"; they were,
rather, acting as custodians of "the remains of old national
franchises", and "if these franchises are suspended, they are
not destroyed". Their example, they argued, was a standing
reminder that subsidies ought only to be levied with the consent of the people. So the King must recall the Parlements

(which Brienne had dismissed) as "depositories of the laws", and summon the Estates General to consent to taxation. A new era would then open, "human nature will begin to regain its dignity, and the people will begin to count for something"; by calling the nation into partnership, the Crown would achieve its highest destiny, for "the glory of your Majesty is, not to be King of France, but King of Frenchmen, and the heart of your subjects is the finest of your domains".

Without honour in the two orders to which he belonged— the Clergy and the Nobility—Brienne hit upon the idea of calling in the Third Estate. "Since the nobles and clergy abandon the King, their natural protector, he is obliged to turn to the commons and use them to crush the other two orders". This is the langauge of a revolution directed by the Throne. A Richelieu could have carried the policy through; in the hands of the court it was to prove a temporary device, a fatal dalliance with the *politique du pire*. Brienne himself fell from power in August, and it was left to his successor Necker (a Protestant banker replacing a nobleman prelate) to double the representation of the Third Estate in the approaching Estates General. Once the opposition of the aristocracy to this doubling of the Commons was manifested, the surge of revolutionary passion swung into a new course—or rather, it became canalized towards its true objective. "A change has come over the controversy," wrote Mallet du Pan in January 1789, "the King, despotism, and the constitution are now secondary questions: the main issue is a war between the Third Estate and the other two orders." The middle classes, with popular support, moved into the attack on privilege. The tension between "royal power" and "the demands of the citizens", which Malesherbes had spoken of, was now absorbed in the overwhelming demand for a juster social order: the fight for liberty was revealed as a campaign within a greater war for equality. This coalescence of the ideas of liberty and equality, the vision of a France in which the Crown obeyed the will of the nation and the manifold privileges of nobles and clergy gave place to the career open to talents and a rationally ordered society, generated an almost messianic enthusiasm, the magic spirit of '89, which lasted for so brief a space, and changed the course of history so decisively. In the limitation of despotic rule, in the abolition of privilege, and in the whole dream of national regeneration, the Church of France was, inevitably, deeply concerned—partly because the Church itself was inextricably involved in the question of privilege, being at once a stronghold of privilege as against the rest of the nation, and a corporation deeply fissured within itself by the feud between its own privileged and unprivileged members.

2. Church, State, and Society on the Eve of the Revolution

In eighteenth-century France throne and altar were commonly spoken of as in close alliance; their simultaneous collapse, said the *philosophe* Chamfort, sardonically, would one day provide the final proof of their interdependence. This alliance, a mystical concept which Bossuet had illuminated with his eloquence and which was brought to earth in tangible form, once in a generation, in the splendours of the coronation, in practical terms was an arrangement giving power and prestige to both sides at no cost to either—except to the spiritual mission of the Church.

Though the clergy were the first Order in the State and all attempts to breach their taxation privileges had failed, the monarch was accustomed to getting his way in ecclesiastical affairs and, within reason, to receiving the subsidies he asked for. The Gallican tradition, embodied in the articles of 1682 and the commentaries of the lawyers, excluded the Pope from intervening between the King and his clergy; papal rescripts and canons of councils could not be published in France without royal approval, and churchmen could not be judged by any authority outside the kingdom. By the Concordat of 1516 the Crown named the bishops and the abbots of the great monasteries, a rich field of patronage which had come to be scandalously used to bribe the nobility into political inactivity. On its side, the Church gained the role of the moral leadership of the nation and the protection of power. In all official ceremonies, from the accession of a monarch to the installation of a municipality, from the opening of the law terms to the execution of a criminal, the Gallican Church played its part,

5

with a mass or Te Deum, a sermon or an exhortation. The registration of births, marriages, and deaths was in the hands of the parish priests. There were ferocious laws against blasphemy and (though there were no actual laws) even more ferocious punishments were imposed by the tribunals for sacrilege. The State enforced the payment of tithe and the observance of monastic vows; the censorship suppressed books dangerous to religion or morals. And above all the "Catholic, Apostolic, and Roman religion" was maintained in its monopoly of public worship. Only recently had the active persecution of Protestants ceased; the last of the women imprisoned in the Tour de Constance were released in 1769, the last pastor to suffer martyrdom died in jail at Meaux in 1771, and the last galley slaves came home in 1775. The so-called "Edict of Toleration" of 1787 did no more for the Calvinists than make their marriages legitimate: it was still illegal for them to meet together to pray. Even so, the bishops (with a few tolerant exceptions, like the Archbishop of Narbonne and the Bishop of Langres) became alarmed, and the Assembly of the Clergy pressed the King to make a "solemn declaration" to maintain Catholicism and never to allow "the public exercise of any other religion".

Of the advantages and privileges which the Church enjoyed as a corporation in the State, only one advantage and one privilege need be mentioned—inordinate wealth and exemption from ordinary taxation. The Church had vast landed possessions, ranging from the garths and gardens of *curés* to the great seigneurial complexes farmed out by bishops and the Benedictine monasteries. Rumour inflated the extent of these holdings, until there were those who believed that they covered a quarter, or even a third, of the whole country. This would be true of Picardy and the Cambrésis and of the area within the boundaries of many towns, but there were tracts in the south where ecclesiastical institutions owned only 3 or 4% of the land, and for the whole of France a modern estimate goes no higher than 6 to 10%. Even so the income from property was immense: a mean among guesses by well-

informed contemporaries would put the annual total at
100,000,000 livres—nearly enough to have paid a living wage
twice over to all the priests of the Gallican Church. And in
addition there was the tithe, yielding a revenue of at least
half as much again.

The central business of this vast institutional patrimony,
more especially the arrangements for voting taxation to the
Crown and collecting it, was in the care of the Assembly of
the Clergy, a gathering of bishops and other high ecclesiastics,
with an expert council of lawyers and two Agents-General,
smooth young aristocrats on their way up to the episcopal
purple, looking after affairs in the intervals between meetings.
If the privileges of the clergy were anywhere threatened—by
municipal officers registering a canon's servant for militia
service, or a prince apanagist reviving an old feudal exaction—
the office of the Agents-General would give legal advice and
warn all the other dioceses to be ready to repel similar
pretensions. Wary and well-organized, the clergy were commonly supposed to evade paying anything like their fair share
of taxation. It is true that they escaped fairly lightly, though
when everything is counted—more especially the contributions
made directly to provincial Estates by the clergy of provinces
annexed since 1561—it is evident that rumour, once again, had
been unjust to them.

Part of the wealth of the Church (a Controller General at
the mid-century conceded that it might rise to as much as sixty
millions) was spent on charity and education. There was no
lay nursing service. The hospitals, refuges of misery beyond
description, were served by nuns, more especially the *sœurs
grises,* the Sisters of Saint-Vincent de Paul. Before the devotion of these women of the religious orders, *philosophes* and
anti-clericals were silent, though—as is the nature of the
case—the poor they served have left no record of their thanks,
while niggling local officials have been able to register their
complaints: that the sisters were too severe on the fallen girls
at the Salpêtrière, that they took the patients' eggs at Amiens,
and put 'immodest statues" on the lawn of their rest house

at the Hôtel-Dieu at Provins. Teaching, like nursing, was
virtually a clerical monopoly under the *ancien régime.* There
were the village schoolmasters, doubling up as clerks, bell-
ringers, and sextons and paid, likely as not, from some pious
"foundation" administered by the churchwardens. For girls,
there were the multitude of convent schools, ranging from
luxurious boarding establishments for the daughters of the
rich to humble day schools for girls of poor families. For
boys, there were something like 560 *collèges,* with their many
free places, within whose walls the leaders of the revolutionary
generation had learnt their Latin themes under the charge of
Jesuits (now suppressed), Oratorians, Minimes, and Maurists;
or, for the sons of the lesser bourgeoisie, the 114 houses of
the Frères des Écoles Chrétiennes, where practical arts were
taught—book-keeping, navigation, architecture, horticulture.
There were, too, the choir schools of the cathedrals and the big
collegiates, from whence came the singers and instrumentalists,
not only of the churches, but also of the theatres and, during
the Revolution, of the patriotic festivals and the observances
of the revolutionary religions.

The chief burden of the work in nursing and education fell
on the communities of men and women which had been
founded in the religious revival of the seventeenth century—
while the great landed donations to the monasteries of France
had been made in the Middle Ages. Those who had come
earliest to work in the vineyard were the first to retire to the
shade, leaving the most useful institutions, socially speaking,
as the poorest. Though there were exceptions, either way, to
this rule, the lack of correspondence between rent rolls and
functions was a disaster for monasticism in a critical, utilitarian
century. In truth, downright scandals were rare, though the
historian can always find a few to liven his pages—a prior
winning a drinking contest, a Cordelier stealing from offertory
boxes, a brother fleeing to Holland with a woman and the
cash box. The declining fervour of monasticism in France was
seen, rather, in numerous examples among the men, of sloth

and preoccupation with the management of material possessions—the drowsy *bonhomie* of isolated religious clubs which
had forgotten the wider patriotism of their Order. Yet it is
impossible to generalize. There were austere houses in decadent
orders and saints in monasteries riven by faction and scandal.
The whole atmosphere of a community might change from
one generation to another. Everywhere there was diversity;
Trappists in life-long silence; Carmelite nuns maintaining
their perpetual devotions; Capuchins on their begging tours;
Benedictines of Saint-Maur eating and drinking heartily as
they toiled on their learned editions of chronicles and the
Fathers; aristocratic abbesses of great Benedictine houses
giving hunting parties; noble canonesses, with their temporary
vows, waiting for handsome suitors to appear; Recollects
winning a reputation for coolness under fire as chaplains in
the army; the Trinitaires negotiating with the Barbary pirates
for the ransom of captives . . . It was a tragedy when this
rich diversity was swept away in an undifferentiated condemnation.

"A monk—what does he do for a living? Nothing, except
to bind himself by an inviolable oath to be a slave and a fool
and to live at the expense of other people." In this case
Voltaire's savage exaggeration did not go far beyond general
opinion. The *cahiers* of grievances brought to Versailles by
the deputies to the Estates General show that the laity were
insisting on some radical reform of monasticism, though few
went so far as to recommend "total and absolute suppression".
On the uselessness of monks the writers of the Enlightenment
were agreed, and their attack received support from erotic
and sentimental novelists, who found in the cloisters the setting for dramas of forced vocations and stifled passions. A
few reforming theorists were ready to see the State take over
the patchwork complex of the charitable activities of ecclesiastical institutions; since La Chalotais' *Essai d'éducation
nationale* (1763), it was commonplace to say that monks had
no stake in the country, and were therefore unsuited to educate
the citizens of the future. As for the contemplative life, its

defenders were few: "benevolence", not "penitence", was regarded as of the essence of religion in the eighteenth century.

Even so, the unpopularity of monasticism in France can hardly be ascribed, in the first place, to the denunciations of *philosophes* and *littérateurs*. In the monasteries the wealth of the Gallican Church, enviously regarded at a time of national bankruptcy, reached its ultimate point of maldistribution and wastefulness. It was here, too, that the operation of privilege in society was seen at its most scandalous—in the *commende*. A half and more of the revenues of each of the great abbeys of France went to the titular "abbot", the abbot *in commendam*— some tonsured courtier free from all ecclesiastical obligations, or an aristocratic churchman drawing a supplement to his income. These abuses were common knowledge since the Commission des Réguliers had been set up in 1765, at the instance of the Assembly of Clergy, which feared that the suppression of the French Jesuits three years earlier might become an example for the destruction of other orders. The proceedings of the Commission had also shown how easily monasteries could be suppressed, without reference to the Pope or protests from the clergy, as well as demonstrating how few would, in fact, be touched, if churchmen were left in charge of the reform. During this prolonged inquisition, municipalities had been encouraged to dream of confiscating convent buildings for orphanages, barracks, schools, or offices for bureaucrats; while the triumphant survival of the worst abuse of all, the *commende,* showed that the grip of the aristocracy on ecclesiastical revenues could only be broken by revolutionary action. Here perhaps is the rare case where one can be specific about the vexed question of the influence of writers upon the events of the Revolution. The *philosophes* did not inspire the widespread criticism of the monks or the envy of their property, but they organized the mass of individual envies and grievances into a theoretical attack upon the whole concept of the cloistered life and the perpetual vows that were its foundation. When abuses were so complex and pervasive, the need for reform so urgent, and the time so short, it was easy for the extreme, the total solution, to prevail.

Except where the downfall of monasticism is concerned, the theme of a war between Church and Enlightenment, central to the intellectual and literary history of the eighteenth century, tends to become peripheral when transferred to the history of politics and society. It furnishes only secondary motives for mens' actions. Though the literature of dissidence added bright satirical foam to the surface swirl of the current of anti-clericalism, this anti-clericalism was surging up from every-day instinctive passions—envy of the wealth, privilege, and political influence of churchmen, suspicion of a celibate clergy and of the influence of the confessional upon the minds of women, resentment of ecclesiastical feuds and hypocrisy, characterized throughout the century in the *déboires* of the Jansenist quarrel, with its formularies, consultations of lawyers, declamations of magistrates of Parlement, persecutions, refusals of sacraments, unedifying miracles. And anticlericalism was part of an accepted way of life, not an inspiration for innovation. Voltaire's exhortations to his "chapel" of *philosophes,* dedicated to crushing the *Infâme,* and the preachers' counter-denunciations of the conspirators against religion, provided entertainment and scandal; but most people could not afford the time to get involved, and the men of leisure who chose to take sides did not propose to inconvenience themselves for either. France was a conformist, Catholic country. Religious practice was never more general, as Gabriel Le Bras has shown, than from 1650 to 1789. It is true that in the towns the upper classes were forsaking the observances of religion: in Paris and Bordeaux, less than half the legal communicants made an annual approach to the altar. In the countryside, however, and in most small provincial centres the Easter "duty" was an obligation except among old soldiers, tavern keepers, members of former Protestant families forcibly "converted" to Catholicism, and the occasional nobleman or bigwig at feud with the local clergy.

It is difficult, perhaps impossible, to assess the degree of fervour, or of positive allegiance to the Church, behind the statistics of conformity. Fasting, pilgrimages, and confraternities were declining. Sermons were becoming more intelligent. The interiors of churches were being adorned with paintings, grilles, baldachins, with marble, stucco, and gilding, amid some destruction of "Gothic" ornamentation which later antiquaries have condemned as an anticipation of the revolutionary vandalism. The cathedrals and richer parish churches celebrated their offices with a magnificence of vestments and ceremony, and a spendour of music, that have never been surpassed. Religion, one is tempted to say, was becoming formalized, excessively decorous. But, before resorting to this facile verdict, one ought to notice that the parish priests were now more respected and influential than they had ever been in ages of ruder piety and more obvious devotion. The reforms of the seventeenth century and the working of the diocesan seminary system had endowed the Gallican Church with a pastorate which lay society could respect—prone, maybe, to litigation over tithes and other dues, and with only a sprinkling of learned theologians, but enlightened in outlook and decent in conduct. The *curés*—whose eccentricities fill the chronicles of the sleepy provincial towns, whose ponderous or piquant style drives home the argument of many a complaint in the files of the intendants, who regale one another with rustic Latin verses in Marmontel's memoirs or, in Besnard's, trudge off to say mass in one another's churches, dog at heels and gun on shoulder— were men of character and leaders of local life. Indeed, one of the manœuvres of the *philosophes* was to contrast the worthy parish priests with the idle monks and canons; the *bon curé*, charitable to the poor, skilled in veterinary medicine, an expert at arbitration and the rescuer of star-crossed lovers, was a familiar figure in eighteenth-century literature. From the *cahiers* it is clear that Frenchmen regarded their parochial clergy with respect and looked forward to seeing them given a fairer share of the wealth of the Church.

An analysis of the *cahiers,* with attention to their omissions as well as to their contents, suggests that, in the concern of most Frenchmen with ecclesiastical affairs, these endowments were the central point of interest. The *cahiers* often ask for an increased income for the *curés,* though, say some, tithe is a burden; given the great riches of the church, say others, surely surplice fees ought to be abolished; there are proposals to take over some of the property to pay off the national debt, to make bishops' emoluments less princely, to end the *commende,* to reform the monasteries and put their revenues to better use, to ensure that ecclesiastical incomes are spent locally, to deprive Rome of further payments of annates and fees for dispensations. There is a financial flavour about all these recommendations, though some of them, it is true, are professed with an envious, anti-clerical gusto. But hardly anyone is interested in freedom of worship for Protestants, or equality for Jews, or in taking away the Church's role in education and public ceremonies. Everyone assumes that the State Church will remain, the Church of the King and of a resurgent nation. Frenchmen tended to anti-clericalism, but they liked the local clergy they knew and retained a respect for their old schoolmasters. Almost everyone had a relative somewhere in orders. Their anti-clericalism had that intimate bitterness peculiar to family quarrels. The shouting would be outrageous, but in the end all the parties to the dispute would have to go on living together. The *philosophes* themselves assumed that, once clerical pretensions had been humiliated, the Church–State alliance would continue, with the sovereign indisputably in command. Voltaire, Raynal, and most of the others cynically accepted the inevitability of ruling men this way, for if the world was released from the meshes of traditionally established faith, what would prevent the servants from stealing the spoons? In 1758, Helvétius had called for the invention of an empirical system of lay morality, "like an experimental physics". But a dozen years later, d'Alembert pointed out that no one had yet discovered how to persuade the poor to be virtuous in cases where they could not be found out—"if I had discovered a satisfactory solution to this question, I'd have long ago written my catechism of morality".

Even to Rousseau, a genius of a finer temper, a state religion was a necessity; he saw the *religion civile* as the heart of the moral machinery by which the inherent vices of civilization could be eradicated. The idea of a lay State and of an independent Church did not enter anyone's mind as a practical possibility.

The almost universal acceptance of the necessity of an official Church serves to define the practical implications of the Enlightenment's challenge to Christianity, not to minimize it. In retrospect, we can see how Buffon was staking out a claim for the autonomy of scientific thought, and how Voltaire's ridicule of the scriptures (brazenly lifting his facts from Don Calmet's innocent commentaries) was foreshadowing the threat of historical criticism to a Church which had turned its back on the researches of Richard Simon. But at the time the most effective intellectual challenge of the writers was their insistence upon a new concept of man and their rejection of certain aspects of the concept of God in the Christian thought of the century. The essential, unifying conviction of the Enlightenment, Cassirer has emphasized, was the rejection of the idea of original sin. That cab-horses are whipped, said Voltaire, is no proof that an ancestor fell from grace by eating forbidden oats. This sentiment met with universal agreement. For once Rousseau was at one with Voltaire, only he rediscovered original sin, not in man, but in society, civilization itself being corrupt and corrupting. Everyone agreed that man had an inalienable right to pursue happiness here on earth. Reason and sentiment, those contrasting inspirations of the age, conspired to proclaim that he was good in his nature and free to seek his own destiny. Enlightened self-interest was the well-spring of moral conduct, and toleration was the first of all virtues. These beliefs constituted the Enlightenment's new doctrine of humanity.

This did not mean that belief in God was abandoned (though the doctrine of the Atonement became meaningless and Jesus was reduced to Socratic status). The main current of thought was not atheistic with d'Holbach, nor deistic in

Voltaire's pessimistic fashion, likening humanity to rats on a ship bound for an alien destination; it was, rather, deistic in Rousseau's sense, finding God in nature and in the noblest sentiments of the heart. If these ardours seem forced to us now, we ought to remember that, at its highest, the deism of the eighteenth century was recalling Christianity to its central doctrine of the love of God, which the theologians had been in danger of obscuring. The *Encyclopédie* article on "Damnation" sardonically rehearsed the "Christian" view: that eternal punishment is "clearly revealed in Scripture", so that it is useless to ask how it can be reconciled with God's goodness and justice. Under the pressure of these criticisms religious apologists were moderating and explaining and ordinary Christians were making their private mental compromises. And so the process of interaction would have gone on, had not the accidents of revolutionary times divided Church from nation and, for a brief, revealing period, compelled deists and patriots to invent their own religion.

At the beginning of 1789 no one dreamt of such a possibility. Unaware of the dangers ahead, confident in their established position in society, the parochial clergy welcomed the approaching meeting of the Estates General. In the great assault on privilege they were at one with the revolutionary middle classes. They complained that they were the workers of the Church, while the drones enjoyed the greater part of ecclesiastical revenues. Chapters and monasteries, owners of broad acres and feudal dues, were the tithe owners in nearly half the parishes of the kingdom, paying over to their *curés* an official *congrue*, a dole barely enough to live on, and enjoying honorific rights in the parish churches which offended the pride of both *curés* and people. There were complaints too of the excessive riches of bishops, of their aloofness, their non-residence, their "despotism", of the higher clergy's monopolization of representation on the Assembly of the Clergy of France; there were suspicions that the richer benefice holders were avoiding paying their fair share of the taxes levied within the clerical Order. Behind these grievances, in all their complex, traditional details, lay one overwhelming scandal, binding all other injustices together into a vicious system of exploitation, and linking the discontents of the *curés* inseparably with the discontents of the nation. Of all the privileges annexed by the aristocracy none was more blatant or more cynically exercised than its monopoly of the positions of honour and high emolument which the Gallican Church afforded. The better-paid canonries and benefices without cure of souls, the abbots' revenues from the richer monasteries, and all the bishoprics, were theirs. Blandly and confidently the younger sons of court families moved into their episcopal sees, often before the age of thirty. Though some showed pious zeal and others administrative ability, it was hard to forget the means by which they had achieved promotion—and a few were openly vicious and unbelieving. "At the very least", said Louis XVI when Loménie de Brienne was mentioned for the see of Paris, "the Archbishop of Paris must believe in God".

From the middle of the century the *curés* of various dioceses had been leaguing together to ask for an improvement in their lot; they protested against the inadequacy of the *congrue* and amassed arguments to show that the tithes ought to belong to them as of right; they asked for representation on the diocesan bureaux which compiled the assessments to clerical taxation, and insisted on the publication of annual taxation tables. Their demand for economic justice more and more became tied up with a movement of theological opinion known as "Richerism"—after Edmond Richer, the seventeenth-century canonist, who had exalted the rights of the *curés* in limitation of those of the bishops. Christ had given a direct commission, not only to the twelve apostles, but also to the seventy disciples mentioned by St Luke—the spiritual ancestors of the parish priests. Bishops then were entitled to a certain primacy, but not to despotic powers. The *curés*, meeting in synod, ought to share in the government of the diocese and enjoy precedence over monks and canons, who exercised "man-made offices" of no account in the hierarchy of the Church.

These ideas of Richer were propagated originally by Jansenist lawyers and canonists as part of their protest against episcopal persecution; soon, however, they became widespread, even in areas where Jansenism was abhorred. *Philosophes* and novelists added their encouragements; the *curés,* said Restif de la Bretonne, are "an order as respectable as it is useful and not given anything like its fair share of temporal goods". By the end of 1786 clerical discontent was general—it was the beginning, in Chassin's phrase, of "the insurrection of the *curés*".

Throughout the next two years the parochial clergy agitated, caballing and pamphleteering. Their reward came at the beginning of 1789, when Necker's regulations for the elections to the Estates General were published. Just as the importance of the Third Estate was recognized by the doubling of its representation, so, in the order of the Clergy, the weight of voting power was awarded to the *curés*—they were entitled to vote individually in their local electoral assemblies, while chapters could send only one representative for ten canons, and monasteries one representative for each community. "By a stroke of the pen", writes Pierre de la Gorce, "Necker had set up a clerical democracy alongside the lay democracy". In the dioceses the campaigns of the last few years had taught the parochial clergy to look to their natural leaders, men like Grégoire, the parish priest of Embermenil in Lorraine, a Jansenist and a Richerist, who exhorted his colleagues not to miss their opportunity. "As *curés*", his pamphlet said, "we have rights. Such a favourable opportunity to enforce them has not occurred, perhaps, for twelve centuries . . . Let us take it . . . so that our successors will not be able to reproach us for having neglected their cause and our own". Everywhere in France, the parish priests dominated the electoral assemblies of the Clergy. From their *cahiers* we get a glimpse of men in sympathy with the national reform movement and willing to pay their share in a fair system of taxation, but anxious, at the same time, to maintain the clerical Order and its power over the minds of future generations through the educational

system and the censorship. The *curés'* own particular grievances against bishops, canons, and monks are embodied,
generally in moderate, indirect terms—that there be a minimum age for bishops, that dignities be reserved for local men,
that long service in the parochial ministry be required for
eligibility to canonries, that residence be enforced, pluralities
abolished, that there be diocesan synods, that *curés* should be
entitled to choose their own *vicaires*.

But the *cahiers,* everyone knew, were of secondary importance: effective action could come only from the actual
deputies who were elected. Here, the lower clergy made no
mistake; of the two hundred and ninety six clerical deputies
to the Estates General only forty-six were bishops, while two
hundred and eight were *curés.* These men, whose consciences
were to bear the brunt of the divisive frenzies of the Revolution, from the start were in an ambiguous position. They
stood for the Church, for the first Order in the State, as against
a nation stirring with rage to end all privilege. Yet in another
sense they went up to the Estates General as the advance
guard of the attack on privilege, the representatives of the
Third Estate within the Clerical Order. A pamphleteer, author
of *Le Tableau moral du Clergé,* hailed them as members of
the Commons:

"It is a mistake to attribute a united *esprit de corps* to the
clergy . . . Why talk of three orders of citizens? Two suffice;
two alone are justified by experience; everyone is enlisted
under one of two banners—nobility and commons. . .[These]
are the only rallying cries dividing Frenchmen. Like the
country itself, the clergy is divided . . . The *curé* is a man of
the people."

If everything had been as simple as this Malesherbes would
have been proved right—religious quarrels would not have
been involved in the Revolution. As it was, the prevalence of
the naive belief that the *curé* was "a man of the people" was
to add bitterness to the strife when the hour of disillusionment
finally came.

3. 1789: May to October

The revolutionary events of 1789 began with a religious procession. On the morning of 4 May, at Versailles, the deputies to the Estates General marched behind a processional cross to the church of Saint Louis—first the Tiers État, followed by the nobles, then the clergy; after that, under a rich canopy, the Blessed Sacrament, carried by the Archbishop of Paris, and finally, the King, wearing the coronation mantle. At the church a mass of the Holy Spirit was sung, and the Bishop of Nancy preached a sermon, full two hours long, to match the uniqueness and dignity of the occasion. An observer among the crowds that thronged the decorated streets, had he been cynical enough, might have observed signs of approaching disharmony in the national unity which these glittering ceremonies proclaimed. The Third Estate, in black and unadorned, resented the black and white satin, gold lace, and plumes of the nobility, while the *curés,* in ordinary cassocks, saw a deep design in the arrangements which put the musicians between them and the bishops, resplendent in their purple and walking alone. This division, said an angry parish priest, was "doubtless necessary to the dignity of prelates, so that distant spectators would not confuse them with the lower clergy".

The Bishop of Nancy's sermon reflected the ambiguous position of the clergy within the movement for national regeneration. He denounced the barbarities of the tax collectors (his words were applauded, in the very presence of the Host), made a daring allusion to the extravagances of the Queen, and an almost subversive invocation of the national will—"*France, ta volonté suffit!*" By contrast he censured the writings of the *philosophes,* insisted that religion must be the continuing basis of the national life, and said that the ending

19

of exemptions from taxation could come about only by volun-
tary renunciations. The clergy stood for reform—but also for
the rights of their order and for their power over the minds
and consciences of men. It was evident that the preacher, like
the rest of the bishops, was an aristocrat, for with remarkable
lack of tact he asked the King to receive—in a nice gradation—
the "homage" of the clergy, the "respects" of the nobility, and
"the very humble supplications" of the Tiers État. In fact
the first objective of the very humble supplications of the
commons was to destroy the orders of clergy and nobility
altogether.

Battle was joined on the question of the "verification of
powers", i.e. of the electoral credentials of the deputies; the
Third Estate, doubled in numbers by the royal regulations,
was determined, from the very start, to force united delibera-
tions in which its numerical weight would prevail. On 6 May
the nobility voted for separate verification by 188 votes
against 47; the clergy also refused to join the commons, but
by the narrow majority of 133 against 114. Throughout the
month negotiations proceeded in an attempt to end the dead-
lock. The nobles were intransigent, the clergy moderate and
fearful. On the 28 May, when the nobles proclaimed that the
distinction of orders was a fundamental law of the monarchy,
the clergy suggested that the three estates might co-operate in
measures to deal with the shortage of bread—a crafty proposal which the Tiers countered by arguing that this could
best be done in a united assembly. At last, on 13 June, three
curés of Poitou—Le Cesve, Ballard, and Jallet—went over to
the Salle des Menus-Plaisirs, where the commons held their
sessions. On the following day, six others, including Grégoire,
followed them; then eight more in the next two days. On
17 June, the Third Estate declared itself the "National
Assembly". The clerical chamber did not meet on the next
day, as it was the octave of Corpus Christi, but on 19 June,
after scenes of confusion, in which the president ended the
sitting and the partisans of fusion re-opened it, 149 votes

were scrambled together in favour of joining the "general Assembly" for the verification of powers.

The crack in the resistance of the clerical order was caused, essentially, by the *curés'* distrust and dislike of the aristocratic bishops. "On coming here", wrote Barbotin, a *curé* from a village near Valenciennes, "I was prepared to believe that the bishops were pastors, but what I see compels me to think that they are mercenaries"—and he went on to talk of Machiavellian politicians in league with the nobility. Sometimes this hostility found bitter expression in the proceedings: the *abbé* Gouttes complained that he had nearly been crushed by an episcopal carriage thundering into the courtyard; *curé* Jallet told the bishop of Nîmes pointedly, "I am poor . . . I have no means of intimidation or seduction". Yet not all *curés* were for joining the Third Estate, and not all bishops were against. One third of the lower clergy did not adhere to the vote of 19 June, and one fifth of the upper clergy voted for it. Lubersac, Bishop of Chartres, Champion de Cicé, Archbishop of Bordeaux, and the bishops of Coutances and Rodez were in favour of yielding, probably for politic reasons. By contrast their ally Lefranc de Pompignan, Archbishop of Vienne, who had had experience of co-operation with the commons in pre-election days in Dauphiné, was actuated solely by peaceable and charitable motives. Since he had been the hammer of the irreligious writers of the century, his defection was a scandal to conservatives: "Monseigneur, after having spent your life fighting the *philosophes,* you have made yourself their testamentary executor." On the other hand the liberal Boisgelin, Archbishop of Aix, one of the first to declare that the clergy had a duty to surrender its taxation privileges, made desperate appeals to his order not to give up its independence—"carrying charlatanry to the point", said an unsympathetic observer, "of pretending to weep bitterly, which made many of the chamber laugh up their sleeves at him".

Even if Boisgelin's style was too lachrymose, his argument was more effective than his enemies cared to admit. The majority which came to vote for joining the Third Estate

was not, in the last resort, so far removed from the opinions
of its opponents. In spite of their differences radical *curés* and
aristocratic bishops were united in a sense of loyalty to their
Order, to the Church, and to its mission to the nation. Many
of those who added their name to the vote of 19 June did so
with no suspicion that the first Order in the state was signing
its own death warrant; they thought that the question of going
permanently into the "national chamber" was still open for
discussion. "There can be no doubt at all", writes Maurice
Hutt, in a definitive study of this day of dupes, "as to what
the 149 had voted to do. They had voted to cross to the Third
Estate's Chamber to check election returns. It was not a
decision to merge the Order with that of the Third Estate".

Events now raced to a crisis: in a week's time the Orders
of clergy and of nobility were to be ended. The commons—
the "National Assembly"—defied the king by the "Oath of
the Tennis Court" (20 June). Two days later, the Archbishop
of Vienne led 150 clerical deputies to join the commons in
the church of Saint Louis, where they had found a temporary
home since their hall had been sequestrated. On 23 June came
the *séance royale*. The "assembled nation" refused the king's
orders to disperse. It is said that about 80 *curés* stayed behind,
in spite of the royal command, but that the Archbishop of
Vienne called them outside, and when they tried to get back
to join the defiant commons, the guards turned them away. On
the following day the Archbishop made amends by again leading the majority of the clergy to join in the National Assembly.
On 27 June Louis XVI capitulated and ordered the first two
estates to join the third. A grim element of mob violence
directed against the clergy had now appeared in the Revolution; on the previous day the Archbishop of Paris was
attacked in his carriage and barely escaped with his life. "*Il
s'en fallut de peu*", grumbled his coachman, "*pour qu'il n'y
eût en même temps deux sièges vacants*".

"The whole business is now over, and the revolution complete", wrote an English visitor, when he heard of the King's
capitulation. In fact, the great drama was just beginning, the

crust of order was breaking, and in the tensions of mob violence at the end of June the idea of using force to settle the political question had been born—first of all in the minds of courtiers, and then in the whole community, as resistance was organized. German and Swiss mercenaries moved in on the capital. On 11 July Necker was dismissed. The Assembly was on the verge of defeat. Paris replied by counter-force, an instinctive rising of all classes. The Bastille fell, and the capital set up its own municipal authorities and National Guard. All over the country the citizens of the towns formed militias to defend themselves against the "aristocratic conspiracy", and against the lower orders who might threaten property if anarchy prevailed. Royal "despotism" was broken. Rural France had been aflame with peasant risings in the Spring and again in late July, as the fear of "brigands" was added to starvation and hatred of feudalism. The towns refused to obey royal officials, and took orders only from the Assembly. In October Paris intervened again to coerce the King. The women and National Guards who marched to Versailles were desperate for bread and afraid of a new military coup, but they were also the agents of a set design, and they brought the royal family back with them to Paris. The Assembly followed there, to be protected and inspired—and swayed and terrorized—by the intensely alert, politically-minded, and anti-clerical population of the capital.

4. The Ecclesiastical Policy of the Constituent Assembly: August 1789 to June 1790

The fate of the Church of France was now in the hands of the Assembly. Its lay deputies were not, as pious legend once had it, a crew of Jansenists, Protestants, *philosophes*, unbelievers, and anti-clericals; in fact, of categories that can be counted, we know that there were only three lay Jansenists (all *avocats*) and fifteen Protestants altogether. "Their most subversive wishes", wrote Dom Leclerq, the clerical historian of the October Days, "did not go beyond reform of the Church". "In the great majority", according to Mathiez, "they were sincere Catholics". When the Assembly declared that it intended to found the new order upon "the sacred basis of religion", it was sincere. The Church was to be a buttress of regenerated France, as it had been of the old monarchy. True the deputies were Erastian and Gallican, as the kings of France had been. They were also men of the Enlightenment, readers of Voltaire, the *philosophes*, Rousseau, and all the rich and reckless literature of dissidence, anti-clericalism, and sentimental deism, and this gave to their nominal allegiance to Catholicism a tinge of scepticism, a flavour of brusqueness. In some respects their policies were entirely predictable, and could have been taken straight from the *cahiers*: the excessive wealth of the Church would be siphoned off, preferably by measures which would alleviate the national debt, the Church would be reformed and the aristocratic monopoly of high ecclesiastical promotion would be ended. Men did not need to have read d'Holbach or the *Histoire philosophique des deux*

Indes to have thought of such policies: they were obvious deductions to anyone who looked at the state of the Gallican Church in the light of the attack on privilege which was the driving force of the Revolution.

An uneasy combination within the same minds of a radical temper and conservative presuppositions bedevilled most of the decisions of the Constituent Assembly about ecclesiastical affairs. What degree of exclusivism, what power over the minds of men, ought to be possessed by an established religion, in an era whose watchwords were equality and liberty? Some of the clergy embarrassed the march of progress by expressing doubts about giving the rights of citizens to Jews and actors, throwing all offices open to Protestants, and lifting the press censorship in matters of religion and morals. But the demand for freedom of conscience was uncompromizingly formulated. On behalf of his fellow-Protestants Rabaut Saint-Etienne objected to the very word "toleration"—"toleration, . . . pardon, clemency! Ideas that are absolutely unjust towards dissenters, if it really is to be a fact that differences of religion and differences of opinion are not a crime!" The Assembly, which put no less than three articles concerning the freedom of the individual into the Declaration of the Rights of Man and the Citizen, hesitated about total religious freedom, and ended up by inserting only a discreet, almost grudging, reference—"*Nul ne doit être inquiété pour ses opinions, même religieuses*", a peculiar formula, invented by a *curé*. Churchmen still felt that dissidents from the national religion ought not to be allowed to parade their nonconformity by public worship and proselytizing. This was why, on 12 April 1790, in the middle of a debate on finance, Dom Gerle, a "patriotic" priest, appealed for a declaration that Catholicism was the religion of State, "with the exclusive right of public worship" ("*son culte sera seul autorisé*"). Not without difficulty the proposal was held up and outflanked, the Assembly refusing to consent, on the nicely balanced grounds that it had no power over consciences and that its attachment to the Roman faith could not possibly be doubted. Numerous deputies

signed a protest against this "national apostasy". In the provinces there was alarm, and indignant meetings were held at
Castres, Toulouse, and Cahors, in areas where the tradition
of Protestantism was strong and memories of old feuds were
unhealed.

The refusal to pass Dom Gerle's motion was not the only
evidence for "national apostasy", for by then the Assembly
had taken ruthless action on both Church property and
monasticism. Everyone expected that the vast, misapplied
wealth of the Church would be subject to patriotic annexations,
though as the real extent both of the nation's indebtedness and
the riches of churchmen were unknown, it was never possible
to devise a well-considered scheme for a loan or a partial
confiscation. Tithe went first of all, abandoned in the delirium
of the night of 4 August. The clergy were prominent in renouncing feudal dues, and the story goes that the Duc de
Châtelet, enraged at the Bishop of Chartres' proposal to end
hunting rights, cried, "*je vais lui prendre aussi quelque chose*"
and added tithe to the holocaust. At the time it was assumed
that feudal incidents were being abolished, but that tithe
would be wound up by purchase. Reconsidering in sober day-
light, the Assembly decided to lay down compensation for the
owners of feudal dues, while tithe would simply be ended.[1]
This was a splendid and scandalous present for a bankrupt
State to make to its landed proprietors.

There was all the more reason now to act quickly about
ecclesiastical property, and in the debate on tithe voices had
been raised proclaiming that the lands of churchmen really
belonged to the nation. On 23 August, the *abbé* Barbotin, one
of the clerical deputies, fearful for the fields and barn of his
cure and his well-stocked pigsty, noted gloomily in his diary,
"They want to put us all on the *congrue*". Indeed this was

---

[1] Given the mood of the Assembly, as revealed in the debates of
10 August, the Clergy renounced tithe on the 11th, and the Assembly
voted that tithe would continue to be collected until an alternative
method of financing the Church was established.

what was going to happen, with the nation paying the salary after confiscating the property. On 10 October, four days after Louis XVI had been compelled to move from Versailles to Paris, a scheme for an "operation on ecclesiastical property" was put forward by a clerical opportunist (Talleyrand, Bishop of Autun) planning a political career based upon collaboration with the inevitable. On 2 November, the Assembly voted by 510 to 346 that Church property was "at the disposal of the nation", which would be responsible for paying the clergy and caring for the poor. "At the disposal of" does not necessarily mean "belongs to", and there was still a possibility that churchmen might retain the ultimate ownership of their lands. On 19 December, however, the Assembly ordered the auctioning of 400 million *livres'* worth. The municipality of Paris, followed by the other municipalities of the kingdom, offered to act as an intermediary in the sales, and by May 1790 the regulations for the vast confiscation had been completed.

Meanwhile the clergy had marshalled every argument against their spoliation. Well-attested donations of great antiquity, prescription going back to the days before the monarchy, the labours of centuries imposed upon the primeval waste (labours arduous enough to meet the conditions Locke had devised for ownership and which *Émile* had made fashionable)—here was evidence to show that the lands of the Gallican Church were property as genuine as that made "sacred" by the Declaration of Rights and owned by members of the Assembly. The sequestration would be accompanied by a wave of corruption; the lands would be snapped up by "capitalists", Jews, speculators; in the end the State would gain as little as Spain had gained by her exploitation of the mines of Peru, or Louis XV from his suppression of the Jesuits. A landowning *curé* had innocent diversions from his studies, a link with his farming parishioners, an extra bond of loyalty attaching him to the nation; a priest on a salary had lost both his independence and his sense of community with lay society. And if war or other disaster came, who could believe that his wages would continue to be paid? Why not, therefore, purge the Church of sinecures and use the resulting surplus income to pay the interest on a vast new State loan?

Patriotic replies to these arguments are revealing. Some have a tincture of vindictiveness—the Church's underpayment of taxation in the past, the superstitious fear of hell which lay behind the original donations, "the immense and careless gifts of our ancestors", said the writer of a pamphlet called *The True Origin of Ecclesiastical Property,* "a foolish tribute paid to a false moral teaching flatly opposite to that of Jesus Christ". Sieyès, who risked his reputation, unbeliever though he was, in defending the Church to which he had given external allegiance, was not far from the mark when he accused the majority of the Assembly of unavowed, subconscious anti-clerical motives. "Can you not forget your animosity against the clergy for a single moment? Is it for us to take our tone from the streets, coffee houses, and *salons* of Paris? Ought we to be stirred by the bourgeois envy that torments the inhabitants of provincial towns at the sight of *M. le chanoine* or *M. le bénéficier*? These miserable [passions] of the private individual are not suitable as guides to our policies. . . . Be legislators, soon enough you will become ordinary citizens again, free to give rein to your hatreds . . . and private vengeances."

As legislators, the deputies of the majority produced arguments embarrassing to Sieyès, for they were based on a political theory and a *mystique* of the Revolution which he himself had done much to create. The new national sovereignty was to know no limitations beyond the rights of the individual, taken in isolation. All powers of the old kings had fallen to it, including Louis XIV's claim that ecclesiastical property really belonged to the State: the clergy were its administrators. Under the *ancien régime* the Crown, of its own authority, had suppressed, united, or diverted the revenues of ecclesiastical benefices: the Assembly was simply doing the same thing on a big scale. In the new State there were to be no privileged corporations to thwart the national will; it was important, therefore, said Le Chapelier and Robespierre, to deprive the clergy of property, so that they could no longer claim to be an eternal corporation, an Order in the nation. This new political theory was buttressed by a new confidence in the movement of history. The eighteenth-century concept of "revolution" as a mere change in the arrangements of government, a turn of the wheel of events, had now been replaced by the idea of revolution as the dawn of a new era. Self-consciously and dramatically the men of the Assembly knew they had crossed over a gulf from the old society to the new, and by the end of 1789 they were commonly speaking of the pre-revolutionary years as the *ancien régime,* a past condemned to oblivion. Yet they were haunted by fears of an "aristocratic conspiracy", of a massing of interests which regretted the past, soon to be summed up in the grim phrase, "counter revolution". The sale of the Church lands was seen as a sort of guarantee that the forces of reaction would not prevail. From the auctions would rise a multitude of proprietors whose interests were bound up with the Revolution, who would fight to defend the new Constitution. A salaried clergy too would be dependent on the new regime. Against the argument that the possession of land is an assurance of the clergy's patriotism, Roederer replied that they must be separated from their "old way of life" and given an interest in the Revolution, "like all other creditors of the national treasury".

One further, obvious reason why ecclesiastical property was sold was that so many people were anxious to buy it. For a long time municipalities and private families had looked enviously on the strategic acres of the Gallican Church, and now the amount of capital available for investment was being swollen by the determination of the nation to buy out all the holders of venal offices. The terms of auction were attractive: plenty of time to complete the instalments, and the reserve prices on the low side, being based on the old leases, which had been easy and traditional. Purchasers with conscientious scruples took heart from the fact that the bishops (with the exception of Cardinal Rohan of Strasbourg) refrained from public outcry. "Our silence", they were to tell the Pope, "demonstrated how we were inaccessible, personally, to all the temporal interests whose possession had drawn upon us hatred and envy". Respectable society led the way in buying—the King's maternal uncle, Xavier de Saxe and, possibly, the King himself, the Duc de Lévis-Mirepoix, the pious president de Chassenon at Poitiers, the future leaders of the revolt of the Vendée, dispossessed canons putting in bids for their old houses, benefice holders trying to rescue some garden or enclosure that had taken their fancy . . . In most places, when the sales opened in December 1790, there was a rush of offers, and selling prices ran at about a third above the estimations.

The effects of this vast auction on the national life and on the course of the Revolution were incalculable. Inventories, sales, hagglings, demolitions; officials, clubs, and committees installed in ecclesiastical premises—all added a faint, sacrilegious perversity to ordinary existence that reinforced the great ground swell of anti-clericalism that was sweeping into the revolutionary events as tempers became frayed over the Civil Constitution of the Clergy. The bourgeoisie and richer peasants who bought most of the property (and did well out of the coming inflation, which reduced the burden of their instalments) became the mainstay of the new order. Here was the "materialistic core of interests at the heart of the Revolution. Ideals which attached themselves to this core could endure, régimes which anchored themselves to it could enjoy some permanence". Sold to meet the deficit incurred by the French contribution to American independence, the alienated patrimony of the Gallican Church was to unite the active and successful groups in French society in their resistance to the kings of Europe, and to embitter the hatred between town and country which played so large a part in the Vendéan rising and in the "brigandage" of the rural populations waging civil war against the Revolution. In the end, the guarantee of this alienation by Rome, in the Concordat of 1801, was to provide the basis for Bonaparte's restoration of the altars and of monarchical rule, while the memories of acquisitions during the great confiscation lingered on in the minds of Frenchmen for long afterwards, intensifying anti-clerical passions and driving political allegiances instinctively leftwards.

Early in October 1789 the tentative decision to sell ecclesiastical property had been taken; at the end of that month of confusion, in which the domination of the Assembly over the future of France had been established by riot, the tentative attack on monasticism began, with the provisional suppression of the taking of vows. The two decisions were connected, for if Church lands were to wipe out the national deficit, the expenditure of the new State-maintained Church would have to be economical. Even so the driving motive was ideological rather than financial. Treilhard's decree of 13 February 1790 withdrew official recognition of existing vows and opened the gates of monasteries for those inmates who chose their freedom. It also distinguished between educational and charitable institutions, which were to remain "for the present", and contemplative and mendicant orders, which were to be suppressed. More than this, it forbade entirely the taking of religious vows in the future. This was ideological legislation with a vengeance, the high tide of utilitarianism and Voltairean prejudice. Full of complaints against monastic wealth and idleness as the *cahiers* had been, scarcely one in fifty had actually proposed the ending of all vows of religion.

Yet it is easy to see how the Assembly came to its extreme conclusion. The excessive riches and abuses of monasticism, the domination of monks over parochial clergy, the tendency of the religious orders to turn towards the authority of Rome, the embroidery of novelists on the theme of forced and reluctantly maintained vocations—the whole atmosphere of opinion had built up to lightning tension, towards trenchant, irreversible reformation. Under the *ancien régime* kings had exercised the power to suppress monastic houses and, on the other hand, had used secular legislation to keep behind their convent grilles all those who had undertaken solemn vows. The new sovereignty was going to exercise all the powers of the old, but loosing instead of binding, and according to a different

ideal of human nature, derived in some respects from
Rousseau, in others from the *philosophes* and from the whole
temper of an age of expanding commerce and more civilized
living. Liberty, happiness, benevolence, utility, patriotism,
were the key words of the century. By them a man was forbidden, however willing he might be, to surrender his freedom
or to rush into unnecessary self-sacrifice; he had a duty to do
tangible good to his fellows, to promote the general search for
happiness, and to serve his country—including, some would
say, an obligation to father and bring up children to its glory.
It was embarrassing, in practice, when a bishop asked for the
name of a *philosophe* who had given away his patrimony to
the poor, as it was three years later when appeals for patriotic
women to replace nuns in hospitals met with small response.
But these were days of regeneration by legislation, and theory
was triumphant.

When, in April 1790 or therabouts, commissioners from the
municipalities went to monastic houses throughout the kingdom, to make inventories and receive declarations of intention
from the inmates, they found, generally, that communities of
women were united in their desire to stay in the religious life.
If certain convents are exceptions, they turn out to be exceptions to prove the rule. In Paris all the houses of nuns
(barring a few individuals here and there) were constant, except the great wealthy abbey of Montmartre and the poor convent of Sainte-Madelaine; in the abbey, out of fifty professed,
the prioress and eleven others wanted to leave, as a protest
against the "despotism" of Mme de Montmorency-Laval, the
aloof and aristocratic abbess, and the thirty-eight nuns who
rushed to escape from the convent were fallen women, who had
drifted into taking vows after being incarcerated for re-
habilitation. The vast majority of nuns remained loyal to their
vocation—in startling contrast to monks, who in large numbers
seized the chance of freedom. There are some obvious practical
reasons for this sharp statistical contrast. Male and female
religious were to be treated very differently; the former were
to be moved off in huddles into a few selected institutions, the

latter were to stay in their own houses and in their own order. Most houses of women did some sort of educational or charitable work, and there was hope that the Ecclesiastical Committee of the Assembly would accept evidence of these activities as a reason for exemption from the decree. It was harder, too, for women to venture out into the world and start life again. There was no place in society as yet for the independent unmarried woman, and "families which had subscribed to endow their establishment in the cloister would not necessarily welcome the return of maiden aunts and elder sisters". Yet, when all is said, the fidelity of the nuns was impressive, and gave the lie to the current assumptions of anti-clerical gossip. "In the world, people like to say that the monasteries are full of victims, slowly consumed by regrets", said the Carmelite houses of the diocese of Paris, in a common declaration, "but we protest before God that if there is true happiness on earth, we enjoy it, in the shelter of the sanctuary".

By contrast many monks demonstrated that they were prepared to seek happiness elsewhere. Perhaps they were in the majority from the first taking of declarations; in the Congregation of Saint-Vannes, the only order for which we have complete figures, 144 wished to stay, 64 reserved their opinion, and 229 chose liberty. It is difficult to contrive a composite picture of what was happening in the various monastic houses, rich or poor, unknown or famous, all over the country. Each community was a microcosm, with its own peculiar atmosphere of devotion or drowsiness, its own internal structure of personal relationships. In some places the hurried gleeful departures of monks and the accusations they bandied as they went are evidence enough of the collapse of their vocation. Yet those who chose to leave were not all such dubious characters as those canons-regular of the abbey of Prémontré, who had already had rehearsals for secular life by sleeping out, going hunting disguised as poachers in black hats, and firing muskets under their Superior's windows. It is a safe assumption that all monks of tarnished morals rushed for freedom—but they were few in number. The much more numerous class of the idle, comfortable, and complacent, was divided. Thus, we may suspect that the departure of most of the inmates of the splendid, great abbeys of Cîteaux, Clairvaux, and Cluny was a token of decadence; yet what are we to make of the Benedictines of Saint-Martin-des-Champs, who slept in four poster beds and as early as September 1789 had wanted to give up their property in exchange for individual pensions, and who yet, in 1790, produced a majority in favour of maintaining their vows? On the other hand, in houses where the rules were strictly observed, there was sometimes a predominance of opinion in favour of freedom. There were in fact arguments, not only of material advantage, but also of principle, in favour of secularization.

Whatever the individual chose to do, it seemed that monastic life in France was doomed to extinction. There was nothing to look forward to but a bleak existence in declining institutions. In the new world that was being constructed by the legislation of the Assembly, the monastic habit would be discredited, and its wearers could have little hope of exercising useful influence in society. The life of prayer, no doubt, was self-justifying, but apart from the Trappists, even the most orderly of the communities of the *ancien régime* had been full of picturesque ramifications that had diversified existence and obscured the claims of pure spirituality. Nor could it be argued that monastic vows were for ever sacred, for the commitment had been contractual, to a particular Order and way of life, and the Assembly had proclaimed its intention of cramming everyone into a limited number of buildings, where separate ways of study, work, and worship would all be confounded. "It is not we who are leaving our Order", said the learned librarian of Sainte-Geneviève, "it is our Order that is leaving us".

Two common replies to the interrogations were—to offer to remain in the religious life, provided there was no question of being removed to another house, or to withold a final answer while awaiting further information. "We cannot state our way of thinking", said the Benedictines of Saint-Nicolas at Angers, "until the houses set aside for us are named, the pensions assured, the rule of life laid down, and until we are told whom we will have to live with and who our Superior will be". An answer could be given to only one of these questions: the religious were being offered reasonable pensions (700 to 900 livres for mendicants, 900 to 1200 livres for others, according to age). It was tempting to close with the offer while it was still open. Obviously, as the statistics illustrate, the temptation was greater for the younger monks, who could more easily start their lives anew. Some of them left the cloister yearning for a more active life, a purpose which was often combined with enthusiasm for the Revolution. Evidence of the "all-or-nothing" temperament which had once led to a renunciation of the world may, perhaps, be seen in the odd way in which some of them—more than one could possibly have expected— turn up later as soldiers or terrorists. It is fascinating to speculate on their careers. What originally led Dom Boniface, the most ferocious of the "de-federalizers" of Maine-et-Loire, into the Benedictine Order, or Jacques Malo, publisher of the newspaper of the popular society of Vire, then *général de brigade* of the Twenty-first Dragoons, into the Cordeliers? A cynic might suggest that their old vocation and their new were alike in demanding a combination of sloth and recklessness. But maybe the explanation is more straightforward and reputable. Men conform to their *milieu,* not only out of self-interest, but also to be well thought of by their families and friends, and even to be of service. The circumstances of the *ancien régime* had made it easy to drift into the monastic round, with a tepid vocation, sincere within its limitations. Once the Estates General met, the whole world was transformed. The national will, the hope of a regenerated society, was calling the monks out of the cloisters—or so it seemed, in those passionate idealistic days before the great disillusionment.

The debates in the Assembly over the legislation on monasticism were bitter. Treilhard's decree, "a decree to proscribe the gathering together of men to pray", was

challenged as an infringement of the rights of the Church,
or even (by the Bishop of Clermont) as the first stage of a
design to destroy the Church altogether. In April 1790, when
surveyors were measuring ecclesiastical estates for sale and
municipal officers were girding themselves up to conduct
visitations of monasteries, Dom Gerle's motion for the affirmation of Catholicism as the religion of State, was put forward—
a demand for reassurance, which was rejected. This "national
apostasy" came only three weeks before the Assembly was to
discuss its Ecclesiastical Committee's proposal for the new
organization of the Gallican Church, the Civil Constitution
of the Clergy. Behind the pomp and speeches which exalted
religion as an integral inspiration of the national regeneration,
coming to a crescendo in the festival of the Federation in July,
churchmen had grown apprehensive and exasperated. Yet there
was still no sign that they might resist the will of the Assembly.
Indeed, the blows that had fallen already seemed to have
hastened the elaboration of a political theory of submission.
Romans 13 applied to the new State as surely as to the old
monarchy. In May 1790 the Bishops of Bayonne and Tarbes
issued pastoral letters on the duty of obedience. It was impossible to approve of the decrees affecting the Church, they
said, but this was not required. A man must simply "submit
his external actions to the established order". Inevitably there
will always be some citizens to whom a particular legislative
act is distasteful; even so, "the common interest" must prevail.
Our duty, said the Bishop of Tarbes, is to obey, and work for
improvements. "Time, experience, tranquil discussions,
moderate petitions put forward by citizens charged with
the duty of making the general will known to the representatives of the nation, will little by little bring about
modifications . . ."

Impressed by such protestations of obedience, the Constituent Assembly settled into a mood of complacent over-
confidence. The gloomy emphasis upon the necessity of mere
compliance ought to have been a warning to its deputies. Sub-
missive in theory, the clergy had now become suspicious in

temper. They had accepted heavy losses at the hands of the secular power, but they would be doubly watchful in future to see that the State did not exceed the boundaries of its legitimate authority.

5. The Civil Constitution of the Clergy

If there was a point at which the Revolution "went wrong", it was when the Constituent Assembly imposed the oath to the Civil Constitution of the Clergy, 27 November 1790. This marked the end of national unity, and the beginning of civil war. For the first time popular forces were made available to the opponents of the Revolution: the Emigration suddenly acquired a conscience. The Assembly, said Alexandre de Lameth, had the recklessness to combine a religious reform with the political, thus creating "a refuge for every grievance", a cave of Adullam to recruit the forces of reaction. Anti-clerical historians-Mignet, Michelet, Debidour, and Aulard—have agreed with this verdict. Mathiez, who tried to switch as much of the blame as possible onto the Roman curia, has also done more than anyone to demonstrate that, so far as the churchmen of France were concerned, the breach was avoidable.

At first prospects for a Church settlement looked fair. Everyone agreed that legislation was necessary, for with tithe abolished and Church property coming up for auction, the State had to make arrangements to fulfil its undertaking to pay ecclesiastical salaries. The abuses of the *ancien régime* were universally recognized, and no one denied that reform would have to be trenchant. There was no support, however, for the extremists of either philosophy or parsimony, for Robespierre's sardonic proposal to choose priests from the whole body of citizens, or for Roederer's attempt to cut down to one diocese for every two departments. An Ecclesiastical Committee, named on 20 August 1789, contained two bishops and three *curés,* and of the ten lay members only three could be described as *philosophes.* By November this body had drafted a moderate plan of reform, which was held up, unrealistically, by the two bishops. Finally, on 5 February 1790, the Assembly added fifteen new members to the committee, mostly men of the left. On 20 May, full discussion of the new committee's proposals began, and on 12 July 1790 the Assembly finally voted the Civil Constitution of the Clergy.

In some ways the new law was well suited to provide the reform which the Church of France needed. Chapters and benefices without cure of souls were abolished; dioceses were to be reduced in number and made to coincide with the civil departments; by suppressions, and redistributions of population, parishes were to be reorganized into a logical pattern. Parish priests were to be given reasonable incomes, graded according to responsibility, from 1,200 livres to 6,000 livres a year. Bishops, constrained to proper residence in their dioceses, would receive a sober income of 12,000 livres, metropolitans 20,000 and the metropolitan of Paris 50,000. Thus the scandalous financial injustices of the *ancien régime* would be ended. The aristocracy's monopoly of promotion would be broken, since bishops would henceforward be nominated by the electors of Departments and *curés* by the electors of Districts. Old complaints about episcopal despotism would be silenced, for *curés* would now choose their own *vicaires,* and every bishop would have to name a dozen or more vicars episcopal, without whose advice he could perform no act of jurisdiction.

What then had the ordinary clergy to complain about? Some thought that the right of departmental authorities to take action against non-resident ecclesiastics was a threat to the "parson's freehold". A minority of *curés,* those with fat tithes in their own hands under the *ancien régime,* stood to lose some income. In towns numerous parishes would be suppressed. As it turned out, at Bourges, only four out of fifteen parishes remained; in Châteauroux one out of four; in Angers eight out of seventeen; in Paris thirty-three out of fifty-two (these figures show the total effect of suppressions and new creations). Redundant parishes were to be abolished without waiting for the death or retirement of their present incumbents—as Grégoire told the Assembly, "venerable old men" would lose their positions of dignity and have to start life again in a society where celibacy and long years of lonely office had deprived them of ordinary friendships: all this for economy's sake—"gold is our God".

It was particularly unfortunate that the Assembly should have ignored the interests of some influential groups among the parish clergy, since practically all of them were reluctant to accept the new method of appointment to ecclesiastical office which the Civil Constitution proposed. Inspired by "Richerist" ideas, the lower clergy wanted election by synods. The electors of the Districts and Departments were a very different proposition. Provided they attended the mass which opened proceedings, Protestants and unbelievers could vote on the same footing as Catholics—in the District of Strasbourg, Protestants would constitute a majority. Thus a *curé* might be appointed by a group of men which did not include a single cleric, in which the bishop was not represented, in which no one had any first-hand knowledge of the parish which needed a pastor, and in which the balance of the vote was tipped by a single Protestant, *philosophe,* or *bon viveur.* Patriots dug into dusty folios to produce examples of the election of bishops in the early Church. "Let us cease building castles in the air: times have changed", a *curé* told the Assembly on 8 June. "By all means let us cast regretful glances back to the virtues of the apostolic age, but let us not flatter ourselves that we will see them revive again in our midst. When the name of Christian was synonymous with that of saint, when the faithful, united by charity, formed one single family of brothers, when their ambitions rose no higher than the yearning for a martyr's crown, then you could have confided to the people the duty of choosing their pastors." A week later he spoke again, describing the debasement of clerical standards which would follow the new system, how *vicaires* would fawn upon the prosperous farmers whose votes could bring promotion, as the English parson courted the squire. But the ungodly had a devastating reply: who chose the clergy before? Bishops and ecclesiastical corporations had exercised most patronage, yet a substantial number of benefices had been in the bestowal of laymen, some being Protestants, and some even Jews. And how had bishops been appointed? By the intervention of valets and mistresses, said Mirabeau, by "odious brigandage" and "obscure and indecent intrigues". Considering the shameless fashion in which the aristocracy had monopolized well-paid office in the Church, it was impossible now to make the blood of the deputies run cold with apprehensions of bourgeois partiality and rural simony.

There was matter for discontent then in the Civil Constitution. Even so the clergy did not dislike it enough to risk repudiating it. There was a majority, even of bishops, in favour of finding some way of making it acceptable. There was one insuperable obstacle. The Assembly was imposing changes without consulting the Church. On two points of detail, the canonists were divided as to the extent of the lay power's competence. The *avocats* Maultrot and Jabineau and Père Lambert (the first a Richerist, the other two Jansenists) denied that the boundaries of dioceses could be changed without the concurrence of the spiritual power; Camus and Durand de Maillane, equally learned in the law, took the opposite view. Canonical investiture was being taken from the Pope: a new bishop would receive institution from his metropolitan, and would send to Rome a simple letter testifying unity of faith. Some of the canonists regarded these formalities as inadequate. And, quite apart from these two tricky points, there was the overwhelming problem of obtaining ecclesiastical approval for the whole reform, taken together. Archbishop Boisgelin warned the Assembly in good time—on 29 May 1790—about "the indispensible authority of the Church". He talked of a national council as one way of proceeding, or of reference to the Pope, without being clear whether the first method would make the second unnecessary.

But one thing was certain: *"il faut consulter l'Église"*. In fact only one method was worth discussion, for the Assembly would not allow a national council to meet, since it would give the aristocratic prelates a counter-revolutionary platform, and would be an admission that the clergy still remained an Order in the State. Only one resort was left. The Pope must approve the Civil Constitution.

The Assembly refused to concern itself with what the Pope might think or do. Such considerations were beneath the notice of the men who were exercising the new-won sovereignty of the nation. "When the sovereign believes a reform is necessary, no one can oppose it", said Treilhard. It was a point of honour with the deputies to be as intransigent with Rome as kings had been. They were heirs of the old Gallican tradition of France; their powers were more valid than those of the Enlightened Despots. Louis XV had suppressed monasteries, Joseph II had overturned seminaries, Catherine II had changed the boundaries of Polish dioceses, and Rome had acquiesced. Regenerated France would be as brusque as the monarchs of the *ancien régime*. So far in the Revolution, the high-handed line in Church affairs had been effective. On 4 August 1789 the payments of annates to Rome had been abolished in a sudden, unilateral decision. Churchmen had remained silent and the Pope had accepted his loss. Sweeping legislation about ecclesiastical property and monastic vows had caused a lot of noise but no effective defiance. The deputies had the impression that public opinion wanted them to press on, without wasting time on conciliation. Ever since they had moved to Paris the laymen in the Assembly had been coming more and more under the influence of bitter anti-clerical propagandists in the capital. All inhibitions vanished from the theatre when, on 4 November 1789 M.-J. Chénier's drama, *Charles IX* was staged. For long it had been held back from production by the pressure of the bishops, but now everyone could go to see a cardinal blessing the daggers for the massacre of St Bartholomew. By mid-July 1790 the anti-clerical theatre had graduated from the sinister to the

lewd—the *Souper des nonnes, Les Fourberies monacles* and
La Journée du Vatican, complete with the Pope dancing a
fandango with the Duchesse de Polignac. By now, there was
savage fighting between Catholics and Protestants around
Nîmes, the outcome of a complex socio-religious feud, which
the press simplified into terms of an aristocratic-clerical conspiracy. This indeed had been one of the main themes of
left-wing newspapers since Easter: that supporters of the
ancien régime were using religion as a stalking-horse for
counter-revolution. The mood of the day was proud, suspicious, fearful, Gallican, erastian, anti-clerical.

Even so the Assembly, seriously concerned to set up a
"nationalized" Church as a bulwark of the new order, would
not have given reckless rein to its prejudices if the possibility
of papal intransigence had seemed a live threat to the settlement. But by the middle of June, the deputies had received
news which made them confident that Rome would yield.
Avignon had revolted against papal rule, and its inhabitants
were asking for incorporation in France. Here was a weapon
of blackmail. It was assumed that Pius VI, a notorious
nepotist, a lover of pomp and a spendthrift builder, laden with
debts, would follow his material interests. Foreign Office experts were set to look up the precedents, and reported that in
1664, when Louis XIV put down a rising in Avignon, the
Pope had rewarded him with *spiritual* compensations. This
would happen again. It was tacitly left to the King to put
through the shady negotiation.

On 22 July 1790 Louis XVI informed the Assembly that he
sanctioned the Civil Constitution, with reservation that he
would be taking measures for its execution; that meant, of
course, that discussions would go on with Rome. The very
next day papal briefs arrived at the nuncio's in Paris, addressed
to the King and his advisors, the Archbishops of Bordeaux
and Vienne. These letters declared the Civil Constitution
schismatic and urged the King to follow the counsel of the
two archbishops (a touch of unconscious irony, for that is
what he had done, and they had told him to sanction the

Assembly's legislation). This muddle and mistiming, this blend of tragedy and farce, was characteristic of the subsequent negotiations. Since the Pope had not made his views public, the King kept the briefs secret, and on 1 August Cardinal Bernis, the French ambassador at Rome, was urged to press for an urgent reconsideration, for the acceptance of some "provisional solution" as quickly as possible. Bernis, a courtly prelate who had been pushed onto the ladder of ecclesiastical preferment long ago by the favour of Mme de Pompadour, made no attempt to hustle. Mathiez describes him as a senile fanatic plotting to become "the Richelieu of the emigration"; he was, in fact, a tired old reactionary who never understood the dynamism of the Revolution, and thought that Church affairs could still be run by intrigues on sofas and in sacristies. While he pottered, events in France were moving fast. On 24 August the Civil Constitution of the Clergy was promulgated by the King. Louis had no real alternative. The Assembly, egged on by one or two deputies who wanted to ensure the independence of Avignon, was restive. Clergy and monks were waiting for their salaries and pensions. The sale of ecclesiastical property was imminent, and no one would buy at the auctions unless the new Church policy was irreversible.

As the sands ran out, the clergy desperately tried to engineer a compromise. The *abbé* Barruel, later to become so notorious in the annals of conservatism, was talking, in his *Journal ecclésiastique,* of "baptizing" the Constitution; *curés* would be elected as prescribed, but bishops would test their fitness and accept them; the Pope would offer his canonical institution to the bishops who were not allowed to ask for it; in exercising their right to choose *vicaires* the *curés* would make a point of consulting the bishop beforehand—in short, without being expressly accepted, the Civil Constitution could be made to work by a sort of parallel co-operation. A number of bishops, indeed, were already assisting in the re-drawing of parish boundaries and were showing a willingness to fit old names to new machinery. The prelates in the Assembly, mostly ignorant of the papal condemnation, helped to draw up the instructions to Bernis of 1 August, suggesting a "provisional solution". On 30 October, Archbishop Boisgelin's *Exposition des principes* (which was ultimately accepted by the whole episcopate) summarized the case against the Civil Constitution in moderate language, and appealed for an eleventh-hour compromise. Let the Assembly suspend the execution of the decrees until the Pope speaks. Boisgelin felt sure that Rome would accept in the end: the Pope's reply could be awaited "with confidence". The bishops, more especially those whose sees were to be suppressed, disliked the new legislation, but they conceded it was viable, provided the question of authority was settled. With the threat of schism imminent, most of them assumed that the Pope would give some sort of consent.

If the episcopate expected Rome to capitulate, it was understandable that the Assembly would feel cocksure. At the very time when the object should have been to get things moving by skirting round the irreconcilable issues of principle, the bearers of the national sovereignty were standing pat on their own unlimited competence. As the crisis approached, there was a temptation to rush matters so as not to appear dependent on a papal decision. A few supporters of Avignon and a few clergy-haters played on this feeling to hasten on a breach. All the while, tension was increasing throughout the country. As the sale of ecclesiastical property drew near, the press accused churchmen of prolonging their scruples to sabotage the auction which they had not dared to oppose openly. As clerical posts fell vacant, the local authorities began to take action to fill them through the new machinery. On 31 October the Department of Finistère elected its new bishop, followed in November by the Ardennes and the Creuse. The *abbé* Expilly, president of the Ecclesiastical Committee of the Assembly, who was elected to Finistère, was flatly refused canonical confirmation by the Archbishop of Rennes. With scarcely any debate, the Assembly passed a curt decree authorizing any bishop to act in place of the metropolitan. Local authorities and clubs began to take the law into their own hands. The directory of the Department of the Aisne declared the Bishop of Soissons dismissed, and the administrators of the Var ordered their clergy to take the oath to the Civil Constitution within a fortnight. On 26 November the Assembly heard a petition from some citizens of Nantes asking for the deposition of their bishop.

It seemed a pity to allow these confusions to continue when the final result was a foregone conclusion. It was assumed the Pope would yield, it was known that the bishops were trying to save the Church from schism and themselves from discomfort, and it was unthinkable that the *curés* would desert the Revolution and wreck the reform which did so much to enhance their status. In a dangerous mood of exasperation and complacency, the Assembly decided to have done. There was an angry debate on 26 and 27 November. When the *abbé* Maury asked why it was not possible "to wait for the reply we have asked for", there were cries of "Are we Italians or Frenchmen?" "We haven't asked for anything!" The debate ended with the passing of a decree imposing the oath to the Civil Constitution of the Clergy on all office-holding priests. This was the fatal moment in the history of the Revolution. "The law of 27 November", said Montlosier, "cut all the bridges".

6. The Gallican Church Divided

The King withheld his approval of the decree of 27 November as long as he dared, and after an unhappy Christmas, finally sanctioned it on 26 December. There was no news from Rome. Bernis had been given a papal note saying that the Holy Office had unanimously condemned the Civil Constitution, but he did not transmit this to Paris until the beginning of January.

Clergy who were members of the Assembly had eight days in which to take the oath. Grégoire led the way on 27 December, and sixty-two followed him. In the next five days there were fifteen more volunteers, one a bishop, Talleyrand, who slipped in quietly at the beginning of a session and got through the formalities with cynical dignity. Only one more bishop of the Assembly became a juror; on 2 January, Gobel, "Bishop of Lydda", coadjutor of Bâle, took the oath, after an odd speech in which he seemed to be making reservations. By two o'clock on 4 January, the last day of grace, Talleyrand, Gobel, and 107 priests had joined the Constitutional Church —about a third of the clerical membership of the Assembly. Grégoire gave a speech appealing to the recalcitrant; they were not required to give interior assent, he said, but simply to promise legal obedience. Barnave grimly asked for a roll-call. It began, amid murmurs from the galleries. Outside, the crowd was threatening vengeance, shouting "à la lanterne". Only one ecclesiastic, a curé, took the oath, and the roll-call was abandoned. There was jubilation when the seventy-year old Bishop of Poitiers came up to the tribune, but it turned out that he merely wished to affirm, for the record, that he "would meet his fate in a spirit of penitence". At five o'clock the president made a last, fruitless appeal, and the Assembly

was left, seething with righteous indignation because so many
of the clergy had done what they had said in conscience they
would have to do.

In Paris, and in many other places, the taking of the oath
was prescribed for the parochial mass of Sunday, 2 January,
the earliest possible date. Elsewhere a later Sunday was
chosen by the authorities, though priests who missed the first
opportunity were always allowed to come in later. National
Guards under arms, martial music, municipal officers in tricolour sashes, packed congregations, including many in-
frequent churchgoers, applause and groans, hubbub and
scandal disturbed the calm of the Sunday services throughout
the month of January. And the result? Out of 160 bishops,
seven became jurors, only four being diocesans. Three of these
were notorious for scepticism and easy living (Talleyrand,
Loménie de Brienne, and Jarente), and one, Lafont de Savine,
Bishop of Viviers, was well-known for his enthusiastic eccentricities. Large numbers of lower clergy took the oath and
large numbers refused it; amid a morass of incomplete and
misleading statistics, the old-fashioned tug of war between
clerical and anti-clerical historians never succeeded in hauling
the totals further than a little way over the half-way line, on
one side or another. We have dubious official figures for forty-
two departments, and incomplete ones for other five, as they
were reported to the Ecclesiastical Committee of the Assembly,
and varying sorts of information about the rest of France;
from this it is possible to obtain a fair general picture, no
more. Some clergy who took the oath retracted, or refused
office, or took office but refused to recognize the new bishop;
some made reservations, which were or were not accepted,
some were put in the lists without their reservations being
mentioned, or even against their wishes; and the numbers of
jurors were swollen by ex-monks, chaplains, private tutors,
and stray ecclesiastics who were not "public officials" and
to whom the oath had not, strictly speaking, been applicable.
Even if we could obtain a satisfactory figure for the total of
jurors (or rather figures; for we would need to know the

totals at different dates), we could never hope to provide comparable statistics for the total of priests who might have taken the oath but refused. There can be no balance sheet of "faithful" and "unfaithful" clergy; indeed, the circumstances under which the oath was tendered were so ill-contrived for honest decision that discussion in terms of sheep and goats has only a limited validity.

The most obvious generalization that can be made about the statistics is also one of the most mysterious, so far as the possibility of a total explanation goes. While in some departments (e.g., the Ardennes, the Meurthe, the Vienne) there was a substantial number of both jurors and refractories, in many there was an overwhelming rush to one side or the other (95% jurors in the Indre, the Loiret, and the Var; 10% or less in the Bas-Rhin and the Morbihan, and less than 25% in the Jura, the Doubs, the Haute-Saône, and the Tarn). The general picture is that the Civil Constitution was accepted in the Centre, the Île de France and the South-East, and rejected in Flanders, Artois, Alsace, and Brittany. There is here a broad coincidence with the pattern of religious fervour as it exists in France today, with "the three great zones of religious practice, North-West, North-East and East, and Massif Central", which Gabriel Le Bras and other students of the sociology of religion have analysed. Four out of every five priests in Brittany refused the oath in 1791: a century and a half later, in 1931, the dioceses of Nantes and Rennes could show 2,079 priests and 422 seminarists as against 932 priests and 94 seminarists for the comparable population of the dioceses of Bourges and Limoges. No doubt the Civil Constitution of the Clergy helped to intensify these divisions of France, but evidence of religious practice before the Revolution shows that they existed already. As yet sociological investigation is only on the fringe of the complexities which must be unravelled to give a complete explanation of this basic phenomenon of modern French history. Fortunately we can attempt to understand the motives of jurors and non-jurors without having to go deeper into this ultimate problem. There was a natural tendency for the clergy to face the crisis of the oath to the Civil Constitution by plans of common action, and where the local population was "churchy" it was obviously easier to stand together as refractories than it was in areas where religious conformity was less rigid and anti-clerical feeling more intense.

The broad tendency (and it was no more than this) towards a refusal of the oath in the traditionally "clerical" areas of France should not lead us to suppose that the arguments for it, on honourable religious grounds, were fraudulent. A priest was asked to swear to be a faithful pastor, and "to be loyal to the nation, to the law, and to the King, and maintain with all my power the Constitution decreed by National Assembly and accepted by the King". Everyone knew that the Civil Constitution of the clergy was included in "the Constitution", but it could be argued that the object was to give a broad, approximate assent to the new order in France. It was a question of accepting the basic nature of the government set forth in the Constitution, not particular laws, said Nicolas Servant, a country *curé* who published a brochure on the subject. Giving a promise "to maintain" the Constitution, said Cérutti, *philosophe* and ex-Jesuit, did not necessarily mean that one approved of it. Cérutti's casuistry was dubious, but Servant's point gained force from the fact that the oath was almost identical with the civic oath of 4 February 1790, which all the ecclesiastics in the Assembly had taken, followed by most of the clergy in the country, including all except two of the bishops. It is true that the Bishop of Amiens had pointed out that this oath might no longer be satisfactory when new legislation on Church affairs was added to the existing fundamental laws—which was what happened, of course. But most of the episcopate considered that it was not the affair of ecclesiastics to go round with lanterns and sticks, prodding the Constitution to find defects. The Assembly's legislation on monastic vows was unjust, said the Bishop of Arles, but it was a valid exercise of sovereign power; the civic oath did not give "interior adhesion" to what had been done, but merely accepted it and promised not to promote counter-revolution. Another prelate, a tough reactionary at that, had issued a pastoral letter saying, "whether a constitution is good or bad, as soon as it is generally desired, it becomes the general rule". When the Assembly had passed the decree of 27 November, it had not forgotten the precedent of the civic oath. Churchmen were to renew their allegiance to a constitution now completed by the necessary provision for a State Church, they were to accept what was "generally desired"; they were to agree, without necessarily approving, that the sovereign power had been validly exercised. The Civil Constitution of the Clergy was being wrapped up in the whole of the regenerated new order demanded by the General Will. It was a package deal that no patriot ought to reject.

There were clergy in France—and their number should not be underestimated—who were dedicated to the Revolution, equating the voice of God with the pronouncements of the representatives of the nation, setting the Constitution alongside the Bible as the token of a new order which Providence itself had conspired to bring to pass. There were many more who, without being so fanatical, were determined on reform, and were willing to take the oath to the new order without dwelling too much on its unsatisfactory stipulations in the matter of religion. After all, the King had swallowed everything: it was "the Constitution accepted by the King". It was assumed that the Pope would yield; he had had time to be fully informed, and no word of condemnation had been published from Rome. Anyway, France was Gallican, and if the Pope was intending to be difficult, there were precedents for forcing him to change his mind.

It is true that the bishops were fussing about waiting for papal approval. But they were aristocrats to a man, unenthusiastic about the Revolution. A simple parish priest who welcomed the reform of France felt less inclined to go out into the wilderness on what, after all, was a mere matter of timing. Even so, as events showed, a bishop who took a courageous line in his diocese could still influence waverers. De la Marche,

Bishop of Saint-Pol-de-Léon, an ex-soldier who organized his clergy against the Civil Constitution as if he was drilling a regiment, and de Cheylus, Bishop of Bayeux, a haughty, worldly old aristocrat, were prickly characters who were not greatly loved, but who had some success because they made a fight of it. Few bishops however were as tough. A dozen, indeed, had already emigrated, their departure, constituting a standing encouragement to the clergy to take the oath out of sheer exasperation. A *curé* of Nancy (whose diocesan was one of the deserters) bitterly and correctly forecast the arrival of a denunciation of the Civil Constitution from across the frontier—"a fine pastoral letter, very learned, very edifying; a new Moses, he will lift up his hands to the sky from afar for the combatants, without sharing the danger". As for the bishops who stayed, though they did not give such scandal, they were mostly no more effective in their dioceses than those who had fled. After inditing a pastoral letter, they remained passive spectators of events. Under the *ancien régime* they had little contact with their lower clergy, and it was too late now for them to don the hairy mantles of prophets to lead a crusade for self-denial.

Inevitably the advice of prelates was suspect to the *curés*. The former had been the beneficiaries of the old abuses: the latter were at last being offered the just treatment they had been fighting to obtain. The Civil Constitution had its defects. The Jansenist *Nouvelles ecclésiastiques* supported it, but the leading Jansenist theologian, Père Lambert of Saint-Germain-des-Prés, wrote pamphlets of condemnation. Some of the Richerist writers were also in opposition—Maultrot, the famous blind canonist, and *curé* Chatizel, who had led the revolt of the lower clergy of Anjou. Yet the Civil Constitution was much nearer to the Jansenist-Richerist view of the proper status of the parish priest than the arrangements of the *ancien régime*. Lay election could be swallowed for the sake of fair salaries, properly organized parishes, equal opportunities for promotion, and the end of "episcopal despotism". Even for

clergy who had taken no part in the revolt against the aristocratic prelates, the pervasive influence of the Richerist argument remained, shedding a dim halo of theological gravity
upon the complex of ideas which made the oath respectable.
Lay election apart, the parish priest was at last getting
something of the place in the hierarchy to which, by a certain
interpretation of the New Testament, he was entitled.

We should remember this when the material arguments for
taking the oath are reviewed: the material benefits came as
part of a reform, as a measure of long overdue justice. There
was a duty to accept them, to brave the inevitable accusations
of mercenary conduct. At the lowest level, of course, there
was the "logic of the cooking pot", for a pension of 500 livres
a year was all the non-jurors would get (and in some places
the club spread the rumour that they would get nothing at all).
The dignity of office and its new, enhanced salary, were re-
wards reserved for jurors. There are stories of priests who
avowed their motives with cheerful cynicism. "You have to
live", said a *curé* of Anjou who, in fact, was an "aristocrat",
an opponent of the work of the National Assembly. The same
formula is ascribed to another *curé* near Evron who was
interrupted in the middle of his oath by the *vicaire*,

"That's not what you said last night."

"*C'est possible, mais il faut bien vivre.*"

Yet, before being censorious about the argument from
starvation, one ought to consider its complexities. *Curé*
Picard of Genouille, near Poitiers, took the oath through the
persuasions of his aged mother, living with him in the presbytery; when she fell mortally ill, she urged him to follow his
conscience, and he retracted. The only *curés* who became
jurors in Angers were two long-established old priests, whose
parishes were to be preserved, with extended boundaries,
better incomes and splendid new churches—the cathedral
and the abbey church of Saint-Serge—for their services. As
parishes were being reduced in number everywhere, a *curé*
had every incentive not to throw away his birthright by
havering and delay. More especially would this be so if there

was a senior *vicaire*, suspected of ambitions, in the offing, hence the anecdote circulating in both Paris and Alsace about the *curé* who rushed back to the pulpit to take the oath once his *vicaire* had done so—"Ah, *canaille*, you think you'll get my parish. But you won't!"

Curé Picard yielding to the supplications of his mother is not an isolated example. Wherever we turn we see family and local pressures operating—sisters, aunts, and aged house-keepers who cannot bear to sell the furniture, fathers and brothers in administrative office coming round with rumours and hints of influence towards early promotion, uncles and cousins who are full of revolutionary zeal and corresponding exhortations, anxious parishioners trying to retain their familiar pastor, local toughs with patriotic menaces and, worse still, fishwives and market women on the war path. There was a riot at Saint-Sulpice in Paris with the cry of *"le serment ou la lanterne"*, and at Sept-Saulx (Marne) the *curé* was shot dead as he declaimed against the Civil Consti-tution in his sermon. To understand the decision of a parish priest one needs to study, not only his own career, but also the revolutionary record of his family and relations, the opinions of his parishioners, and the state of local popular feeling for or against the Revolution.

All these pressures, and others peculiar to their unhappy, uprooted state, affected the numerous monks who volunteered to take the constitutional oath. They were adrift in an alien world, their vows were no longer recognized; those who had chosen to leave their monasteries on a pension were facing a new life in an unsympathetic society; those who wished to maintain their vocation were doomed to be packed into a few colourless, crowded institutions. The idea of well-paid office and, still more, of an assured status in society, was particularly attractive to them and in the predominantly non-juring areas appointments as *curés* or *vicaires* were there for the asking. At the end of 1792 the District of Lille still had only seventy-four jurors for 126 parishes, and called in twenty-four monks from other dioceses; even in Paris, out of 419 constitutional clergy in office in July 1791, 126 were regulars. Until lately historians have tended to assume that ex-monks flocking in for jobs must have been something of a rabble. A recent survey of the 155 regulars of Paris known to have taken the oath shows how easy it is to be mistaken. Previous masonic affiliations, Jansenist leanings, and (what is very different) scandalous conduct or discontent with the monastic life have no obvious connexion with the decision. In 1790, fifty-three of the future constitutionals had refused to accept the offer of freedom from their monastic vows; they had elected to stay in the common life, or had reserved their opinion. Younger monks, rather than older, tended to join the Constitutional Church—this is one of the few generalizations that can safely be made. The wide spread of jurors over different houses and orders (there are some almost everywhere) shows how highly individual the decision must have been; by contrast, the peculiar concentrations that occur show that it was the particular house, as against the Order, which was the unit marking the boundaries of the process of discussion. In a crisis men seek familiar faces and the advice of old friends. The Cordeliers of the Ave Maria convent acted together so that they could take over the vacant parish of Saint-Paul; of the canons-regular of Sainte-Geneviève, few took the oath in the main house, but many did so in a separate priory; in one of the two houses of the Prémontrés the prior published a Richerist defence of the oath and carried most of his colleagues with him, while in the other, out of sixteen canons-regular there were only two jurors, and they had been recently accused of "having received a prostitute in the parlour". We do not know how these two shady characters turned out, but among the Parisian monks there are four or five cases of dubious individuals who took the oath and thereafter proved themselves exemplary—or at least, courageous—priests. In the crisis they seemed to have at last found their vocation. The monks of eighteenth-century France were spoken of with contempt by *philosophes,* by laymen, and even by the parochial clergy. It is not surprising that some of them should have sought to prove themselves (and enjoy office, of course) in the parochial ministry. The admixture of injured pride and self-interest does not make the basic motivation unworthy.

When the case for the constitutional oath is reviewed, it is easy to see how the Assembly could have been so complacent. It is easy to feel, too, the anguish of the non-jurors who considered themselves obliged to refuse it. For them—and it is greatly to their honour—the issue was one of grim simplicity. Only a few would have felt that the actual defects of the legislation (lay election and so on) were a decisive reason to withold allegiance. *"Il faut consulter l'Église."* The Church had to consent to the changes. It was as simple, and as difficult, as that. By haughty mismanagement, the Assembly had deprived the clergy of the chance to make a straightforward decision on the content of the new Church reform. Everything had been made to depend on the question of authority: the whole issue had been precariously balanced on the knife-edge of principle.

Here was a problem on which theological advice was needed, and there was much consultation of local pundits. We can trace how little groups of ecclesiastics were influenced by some neighbouring doctor of theology, some laureate of a provincial academy, or by contacts with the diocesan seminary. In southern Anjou, the "Mulotins" of Saint-Laurent-sur-Sèvre, a group of fanatical missioners, dominated opinion in the countryside. The startling contrast between the departments of the Moselle (28% jurors) and the Meuse (79% jurors) seems explicable only in terms of the Jansenist—Richerist theology taught in the old diocese of Verdun, to which the latter department approximated. To a man the Sulpiciens refused the oath, and their seminaries throughout the country were strongholds of resistance. At Reims their influence over the younger clergy can be seen, as contrasted with the older priests, who had been trained in the days before the Sulpiciens took over theological training in the diocese. On the other side Gratien, superior of the seminary of Chartres, Remacle

Lissoir, abbot of Laval-Dieu (Ardennes) and learned *curés* like Philbert of Sedan and Gervaise de la Prise of Caen were responsible for that touch of theological expertise and respectability which swung numerous waverers into the Constitutional Church.

The objection to the oath on grounds of "authority" was quickly and generally recognized in clerical areas. Here the pressures of family and locality, so often "revolutionary" elsewhere, might tend in a conservative direction, so that a priest would sense that the oath was impossible before he had looked up the Epistle to the Hebrews or the Council of Toledo. Convents of nuns, already scandalized and panic-striken by the revolutionary legislation, often led the way in crying heresy and impiety against priests who proposed to throw in their lot with the State. In the diocese of Dol there is a case of the municipal officers offering the oath to their parish priest then rebuking him when he took it, and of a sexton who rushed into the pulpit to denounce the *curé* for apostasy. Sometimes, especially in a clerical area, the whole parade of mayoral rhetoric and too-evident persuasion made churchmen feel that to yield would be degrading—like *curé* Robin of Angers, who said that his conscience did not need enlightening by the brothers Delaunay, "to whom he had never been able to teach the catechism".

In Angers and elsewhere pious forgers had been at work fabricating a "papal" letter condemning the Civil Constitution. Few were deceived by the forgeries; on the contrary, for most refractories the agony of refusal was intensified by the apprehension that the Pope's sanction would arrive in the usual leisurely Roman way, but too late to leave any jobs for the non-jurors. Meanwhile, the delay in the arrival of the Roman verdict was bewildering: so too was the pressure of an immediate decision in which, either way, a man was compelled to imply more than he intended. Nobody wanted to betray the Church. On the other hand, though the rising furore of anti-clericalism caused alarm, few really wished to desert the Revolution. Jurors and non-jurors alike were acting provisionally, hoping that someone in authority would find a compromise, authorize a delay. In the confusion, it was comforting to consult together, and to stick together on one side or another of a baffling dilemma. In this way, in any particular "natural" grouping of clergy, a majority would tend to become a large majority. In sizeable towns, where good theological advice was available and it was possible to remain in contact, haunting the cowardly, and satisfying oneself of the honesty of other people, the oath was usually rejected. There are few parish priests or *vicaires* among the jurors in Lille, Angers, Arras, Aix, Bayeux. Caen, Falaise, Boulogne, Montpellier, Bourges, Strasbourg, Rennes, Bordeaux, Nîmes, Nevers. As the heart of the Revolution, Paris was an exception; here twenty-four *curés* took the oath and an equal number refused. So too was Orléans, where most of the clergy followed the example of Bishop Jarente, one of the few jurors in the episcopate. These are exceptions that prove the rule. In most provincial towns, the non-jurors were clinging together with reluctant heroism, consoling themselves with the hope that, so long as they remained united, some compromise would have to be found. "This uniformity of conduct in the whole body", wrote a *vicaire* of Angers, "will bring about the salvation of all its members". There was, too, the point of honour. The *abbé* Veri, who had long ago given up his sacerdotal functions, declared that the oath was impossible because it involved abandoning colleagues—"whoever betrays the duties of fraternity is the most infamous of men". The statistical geography of the oath in one department reveals that clusters of constitutional priests consist of average samples of the clergy, while the odd isolated juror in a refractory area tends to be a doubtful character. Could this be an illustration of Veri's proposition?

One way out of the agonizing dilemma was to show loyalty to both Church and Revolution, and to take the oath with restrictions. At Nancy, Besançon, in the District of Revel (Toulouse) and elsewhere, the clergy got together to devize a common formula. In the north the vicars general of Tournai laid down a form of words for the priests of the French parts of the diocese. Elsewhere a great deal of individual ingenuity was displayed; the oath was wrapped up in long discourses, references to the rights of Caesar and of the Church were interpolated, parallel allegiance was sworn to the "Catholic, Apostolic, and Roman religion" or to the Holy Spirit. Municipal authorities made astonishing decisions as to which attempts qualified and which failed. A *curé* got away with references to the authority of the Church, "out of which there is no salvation", and a *vicaire* with a malediction upon himself if he was accepting anything contrary to dogma (though this was logical, for why should the State care if his "hand withered and his tongue clove to the roof of his mouth"?) Others who piled on patriotic sentiments and almost took the oath were dryly noted down as "*Réfractaire*" or "*Déchu, à remplacer*". The Besançon formula, "as and as much as the Catholic . . . religion permits" was thrown out only because of the "as much" clause. Some authorities blandly omitted the *curés'* restrictions from the record; in the Poitiers area three parish priests registered the fact before notaries. Everywhere there was confusion; pottering evasion by the clergy matched, quite often, by fumbling connivance on the side of officials, all in the hope that the Assembly would relent or the Pope prove amenable.

On 21 March the nuncio at Paris handed to the Government a brief condemning the Civil Constitution of the Clergy. It was kept secret, but on 4 May the Pope himself published it. Then came a rush of pathetic retractions. It had been a sad, cruel business.

In spite of the harsh confusions of its origin, the new Constitutional Church was quickly established. In clerical areas, comic anecdotes about its hastily conscripted personnel went the rounds—an episcopal vicar who took his exercise on a treadmill, an assistant priest who said the *Requiescat in pace* instead of the Gloria to the Magnificat. Pious wits had lots of fun over the elections of the new bishops—candidates modestly surprised reading speeches of acceptance from papers in their hats, voters putting ballots in the urn for the Devil or the Grand Turk. More seriously, parishioners loyal to their old *curé* would give his successor, the *intrus,* a violent reception; like those of Malay in Southern Anjou, where the ladies stoned the *abbé* Thubert, "some even going so far as to kick his backside, and threatening worse still if he dared to reappear on All Souls' Day". Women led the tumults: Sicard's history has a whole chapter on their riots. Yet somehow the parishes were filled, quite often with excellent choices. The new bishops were worthy. An unsympathetic historian admits that out of eighty constitutional bishops, less than thirty were unsatisfactory, and proves the honest intentions of the electors by sardonically pointing out that six priests who were offered the mitre actually refused. Of those who accepted, Grégoire, Le Coz, and Charrier de la Roche had outstanding talents, and others were sound theologians and men of character. The question of their consecration might have been difficult, but Talleyrand agreed to provide the link with the episcopal succession—the last time, until the famous deathbed scene of forty seven years later, that he exercised his rights as a bishop.

There was bitterness between refractories and constitutionals. Yet, in the chronicle of petty meannesses, there were exceptions. Some of the old bishops left without reproaching their supplanters, and some of the constitutional bishops attempted to protect non-jurors in their dioceses. At Couteville, near Honfleur, the old *curé* and the new lived together in fraternity for twenty years, and asked in their wills to be buried together. In the parish of Neuville Vitasse, near Arras, relations began in charity. "You are a priest, just as I am, my dear Sir", said the constitutional *curé*, encouraging his predecessor to go on saying mass in the church. "It matters little to the Supreme Being that we do not agree over words, provided we both strive to glorify him by our conduct". Then came the affair of breaking open the sacristy cupboard, and a great lawsuit. Still, the original gesture had been handsome, and it came from Joseph Lebon, the future terrorist.

7. *The Beginning of Persecution, January 1791 to September 1792*

In theory, non-juring priests, having led their flocks out of the well-hedged pastures of the State Church, were now free to browse them inexpensively on the weedy commons, under the protection of the liberty guaranteed by the Declaration of Rights. On 11 April 1791, the directory of the Department of the Seine made regulations to ensure fair play: individual citizens were to be entitled to hire church buildings where nonconformist Roman Catholics could assemble. By a decree of 7 May, the Assembly confirmed this tolerant gesture and added a rider allowing non-jurors to say mass in constitutional churches. In practice, these liberal provisions proved unworkable in many places, for the refractory priests were regarded as traitors to the Revolution, and club members were ready to lead riots to disperse their congregations. The Assembly itself deserves a share of the blame for what was happening. By holding a roll-call of its clerical deputies on 4 January with a raging mob outside, it had already made the oath to the Civil Constitution into a test of patriotism, and it went on to knock a further breach in the Rights of Man by a decree of 25 January which took cases concerning the enforcement of the new ecclesiastical polity out of the jurisdiction of the ordinary courts, leaving them to the municipalities and the directories of Districts and Departments. This legislation, in a sense, marks the beginning of the sinister concept of "suspects". It made the refractory clergy liable to extra-legal administrative bullying in the interests of keeping the peace or of getting the new constitutional clergy established. Thus the Department of the Loir-et-Cher turned out its old bishop at two days notice when the new was expected, and the municipality of Cahors expelled all refractory priests from town within twenty-four hours.

On 18 April, the police, tired of keeping rioters at bay, closed the chapels of four Parisian convents used by refractories. Three days later the King tried to drive off to Saint-Cloud to receive Easter communion from the hands of orthodox priests, but his carriage was turned back by angry demonstrators. With their elemental but shrewd political instinct, the people of Paris had scented danger. A few weeks later, when a guy of Pope Pius VI was consigned to a bonfire, a placard around the neck bore the legend "Fanaticism, Civil War". They blamed religion for breaking national unity, and they feared that the King was going to use the divisions of France to restore the *ancien régime*. On 20 June the royal family fled from Paris; caught at Varennes, they were brought back into the capital as prisoners, amid a glacial silence. Fears of military conspiracies, of an Austrian invasion, swept the country. In various departments, local authorities interned non-juring priests as part of their security measures. In Maine-et-Loire refractories were concentrated in the town of Angers under surveillance, and some were imprisoned in the Little Seminary, while women who mocked at the Constitutional Church were whipped. On 4 August a proposal was made to the Assembly for a general decree arresting all refractories, but such an affront to liberty was, as yet, unacceptable. Two days later Barnave protested against the idea of new proscriptions, and hinted that the logical conclusion of further illiberal measures would be the confiscation of property. "What new night of the 4 August is left for you to proclaim? It is . . . time to end the Revolution." In October André Chénier published an article in the same vein. "Will you let it be said by malicious tongues that in France all religions are tolerated—save one?"

The Constituents had achieved a weary awareness of the

danger involved in legislating on religious matters. By making themselves ineligible for the succeeding Legislative Assembly, they ensured that this expertise was wasted. On 1 October 1791 the new Assembly began its sessions. Many of its deputies had come up to Paris fresh from District or Departmental administrations, itching with anti-clerical vexation at the insults and tumults they had endured over the Civil Constitution of the Clergy. Whatever its mistakes, the Constituent Assembly, inheriting the full clerical membership of the Estates General, had never been allowed to forget the importance of ecclesiastical affairs, and had never lacked eloquent and expert advice about them; the new assembly contained only twenty clergy, all jurors, few of them courageous. Church matters suddenly seemed to be revealed as a subordinate branch of the national administration. One or two of the clerical deputies, embittered by the constant denigration of their motives by the orthodox, were uncharitable enough to propose that pensions be withheld from their former colleagues, the non-jurors—"You don't pay your enemies to wage war upon you". The religious schism came to be spoken of in crudely political terms, "patriots" on one side, "aristocrats" on the other. Among the reckless young Girondins the clichés of division were replacing the comfortable circumlocutions which had once fostered the illusion of unity. Guadet in the Jacobins told Robespierre that he saw "no sense" in the idea of Providence, and Isnard urged the Assembly to amputate the "gangrened limb" of dissidence without delay. Continued opposition to the Civil Constitution of the Clergy in the provinces led the Legislative Assembly finally to pass the decree of 29 November 1791, by which non-juring priests were made "suspects", that is, liable to expulsion from communes where troubles occurred. The King vetoed this measure of exception, along with others against the émigrés, an unfortunate conjunction. Patriots grew exasperated.

War was declared against the "King of Bohemia and Hungary" on 20 April 1792. This was the second of the two great blunders of the Revolution (the enforcement of the oath to the Civil Constitution had been the first). It could be that in the end some kind of schism, some kind of war, were inevitable. We can never know. But at least they could have been delayed, and delay might have saved the Revolution from the peculiar conjunction of threatening events that led to the Terror. The war came when it did because, for contradictory and selfish reasons, so many people were willing to risk it. Politicians wanted a war to coerce the King and sweep them into office; generals so that they could dictate to the capital with armies at their call; the King, to bring his people humbly back defeated, to their dynasty; the Queen, to provoke the foreign intervention she had been unable to negotiate; idealists like Mme Roland, because they had succumbed to apocalyptic visions of regeneration by bloodshed; the masses because they feared the conspiracy of aristocrats, émigrés, clergy, foreign despots and the Crown itself, and had the crusading belief that a nation in arms would be invincible.

With the coming of war, the non-jurors became victims of the full tragic weight of the two great mistakes of the Revolution, coalescing to destroy them. They had refused to join the Constitutional Church, hoping against hope that the schism would be patched up. As Boisgelin said, they had simply done what they were entitled to do, refrained from taking an oath, accepting the consequent deprivation of office, which was supposed to be the only penalty. But now they found that what they had done was taken as treason to the nation. They were regarded as a "fifth column" in league with the Emigration and the invader. The *abbé* Maury, who was made a cardinal by Rome soon after the war began, visited the émigrés at Mayence and declared that the Pope needed "their sabres to trim his pens". This was precisely what everyone believed at Paris. On 26 May 1792, with the shadow of defeat creeping nearer, the Legislative passed a savage decree: every refractory priest who was denounced by twenty "active" citizens would be deported. The King refused his sanction, and thus hastened his own ruin. Meanwhile the authorities in the departments were arresting priests or restricting their place of domicile. On 20 June, a popular insurrection invaded the Tuileries; at the beginning of July Prussia entered the war; on 10 August came the fall of the Throne.

With the end of the monarchy, the deportation decree became immediately effective. On 14 August it was rendered even more stringent; denunciation by six citizens out of the whole department was enough. This was tantamount to a universal proscription, for as things were a quorum could be found to denounce anyone. From now onwards, non-juring priests, unless they were too old for deportation, had to go "underground" if they wished to escape internment and exile.

The deportation laws were unsatisfactory, not only because they were unjust, but also because they contained some odd loopholes. So, before August was out, a new oath was devised, to be taken by all priests on penalty of loss of place or pension, together with deportation if six citizens added their denunciation (on 23 March 1793, a further law made the deportation automatic). The new oath said nothing about the Civil Constitution of the Clergy. "I swear to be faithful to the Nation, to maintain with all my power Liberty, Equality, the security of persons and property, and to die, if need be, for the execution of the law." By our standards of common sense, an oath in these colourful terms is astonishing. It is not a promise to accept, to obey, or to refrain from causing trouble to a government: it is a proclamation of ideological self-identification, a sort of subscription to, and an admission of, the rightness of a Rousseaustic General Will. Royalist pamphleteers argued that such an oath was inadmissible to all except fanatical revolutionaries. They cited the principle of casuistry laid down by St Augustine, that a man swears, not in accordance with what the words might mean, but "in the terms and in the intention of whoever is imposing the oath"; in this case, they said, the intention must include the whole religious policy of the Revolution.

Fortunately, M. Emery, the Superior of the seminary of Saint-Sulpice, a tough and spiritual man to whom fear was unknown, and himself a royalist so far as political conviction was concerned, took the lead in recommending acceptance. It was unreasonable, he said, to await the Pope's ruling. Individual refusals would mean starvation for priests and nuns who depended on their pensions, and a general refusal would mean the end of the orthodox Church in France. The royalists were too obviously anxious to have religion persecuted to make their enemies unpopular. If the point of the oath was to separate Christianity from counter-revolutionary intrigues, it was legitimate. To fulfil the Augustinian ruling about interpretation, Emery submitted an essay on the meaning of the oath to Gensonné the *rapporteur* of the law, and got his agreement that this represented the intentions of the legislature—that "liberty" meant, not a capricious freedom of action, but "government by the laws", that "equality" went no further than equality of opportunity and absence of privileges, that the "law" for whose execution a man might die meant decrees concerning liberty, equality, and the security of persons and property (an enumeration which carefully omits religion), and that to be willing "to die" meant that officials had to act with "ordinary courage", and citizens with "submission and obedience". It was a masterly exercise in intelligent deflation—if only someone in Rome had been working in this way on the Civil Constitution of the Clergy a year ago!

While Emery was coolly defining the concepts of liberty and equality with the disillusioned realism of the professional casuist, the world around him had gone mad. On 1 September news arrived in Paris of the fall of Verdun. It was the last fortress between the capital and the Prussian infantry. At four o'clock the next day, the prison massacres began, a crime of mass complicity. The brutal few (most of them ordinary middle-aged tradesmen and the like before this day of madness) did the deeds, while the many averted their gaze and passed by on the other side. If the aim was to extirpate traitors behind the front as the volunteers went up to the line, the definition of potential traitor was wide; among the 1,400 victims were political suspects, aristocrats, prostitutes, children, ordinary criminals, and ecclesiastics. Three bishops and two hundred and twenty priests perished. There was nothing accidental about their deaths; indeed, the killings began with the slaughter of twenty priests who were noticed by a mob as they were being brought in carriages to the Abbaye prison. Yet they were not the victims of an anti-clerical conspiracy. The story of their deaths, until recently universally accepted by historians of both right and left, was that the murderers set up *ad hoc* "tribunals" and asked one question of all ecclesiastics: *"as-tu prêté le serment?"* The difficulty with this account always has been that we have the word of M. Emery that many of the imprisoned priests had agreed that there was no insuperable difficulty about the oath of Liberty–Equality, and it has now become evident, from the researches of M. Plongeron, that the whole tale of tribunals and oaths is unreliable—a few individuals, perhaps, were asked about the oath, no more. Emigrés and counter-revolutionaries anxious to annex these unhappy victims as martyrs for their cause, have succeeded in imposing their slanted version upon posterity as well as on their own contemporaries. The true story of the massacres is, in some ways, sadder than the legend about heroic martyrs dying because they refused a republication oath (or because they thought that the oath included a belated acceptance of the revolutionary church settlement). The murdered priests had exercised the power of choice more than a year ago, when (as they were fully entitled to do) they had refused to enter the Constitutional Church. From then onwards, they had been trapped in a monstrous procession of events; they had become smeared with suspicions of treachery which they had no means of refuting.

8. *The Decline of the State Church and the Origins of the Revolutionary Religion 1789—September 1792*

The great outburst of reforming and patriotic enthusiasm of 1789–90 had expressed itself in appropriate symbols and ceremonies. In face of an "aristocratic conspiracy", the machinations of a "German committee" around the Queen and the ill will of foreign "despots", and amidst fears of anarchy and the danger to property that would ensue, the supporters of the new order felt obliged to manifest their solidarity—to outfront scheming enemies, convince wavering friends, and inspire all patriots to the utmost self-dedication to the cause of freedom. From the storming of the Bastille, the tricolour cockade combining the white of the Crown with the red and blue of the city of Paris, became a necessary item of dress; later on, an enthusiast could choose to add the *bonnet rouge,* the Phrygian cap which in classical antiquity had been the token of enfranchisement from slavery. The custom of swearing to defend the new order and to "live free or die" arose, unprompted by official orders, in January 1790; the mania for solidarity, manifested throughout the Revolution in the imposition of successive oaths which were to lay so heavy a burden on consciences, had a spontaneous social origin. About the same time, a certain Cadet de Vaux was erecting an embellishment to his country house more serious in intention than the usual eighteenth-century "folly"—a patriotic altar, adorned with Roman axes and fasces, a pike crowned with a cap of liberty, a shield with a portrait of Lafayette, and panels engraved with verses from Voltaire. This novel fancy was copied all over France in the next few months. Meanwhile, imitations of the Tables of the Law found in churches were being made, setting forth, not the Decalogue, but the Declaration of Rights. A *curé* of Poitou planted a "Tree of Liberty", the first of a whole forest all over the country, in May 1790. Two months later the fashion for "civic baptisms" began; a church ceremony but with National Guards forming a sword arch, a cockade conferred as well as the sign of the cross and, sometimes, the infant burdened with a name like *Civique Fédérée*.

All this patriotic symbolism was brought to a focus in the festival of the Federation, 14 July 1790. In almost every town and hamlet the people came together around an *autel de la patrie* to take the oath of loyalty and sing the Te Deum. At Paris representatives of all eighty three Departments attended a huge demonstration in a specially constructed amphitheatre in the Champ de Mars. Here Talleyrand said mass and blessed the departmental banners (and had a private celebration of his own that night by twice breaking the bank at a gaming house). There are few records of cynical comment to mar this vast, unselfconscious enthusiasm, though there are some—Talleyrand's "Don't make me laugh", and the canons of the cathedral of Angers objecting to a Te Deum "on a Champ de Mars, alias the fair ground". The Federation generalized some customs already existing, and added new ones. During the work on the amphitheatre in Paris, one of the revolutionary "hymns", the *ça ira*, was composed, and the banqueting and dancing in the streets was accepted as an observance of the new era of fraternity. *Curé* Dolivier of Mauchamp (Étampes) published a pamphlet urging his fellow citizens to make the communal meal an institution of true equality, where rank would be forgotten, the only places of honour being those reserved for the aged. His proposal accorded with the times, and future ceremonies of the Revolution were usually fortified by "civic banquets", though few were so austere or egalitarian as *curé* Dolivier would have desired.

With the Federation France acquired a standardized brand of revolutionary pageantry, which was adapted as required by local authorities for parades of the National Guard, elections and municipal occasions, and by theatre managers, to produce dramas whose manifest tedium remains an overwhelming proof of the fervour of the patriotism which originally applauded them. Fortunately however, for those who savour the picturesque side of history, the ceremonies of regenerated France did not remain fixed at this level of banality. The procession of 11 July 1791, which escorted the remains of Voltaire to the Panthéon, was the first instance of a collaboration of genius— J.-L. David the artist, M.-J. Chénier the writer, and Gossec the musician. Before the Revolution, David had chosen subjects for his paintings to glorify "republican" virtues—the oath of the Horatii, the death of Socrates, the lictors bringing back to Brutus the bodies of his sons; now he imposed upon the revolutionary processions the costumes and decorations of classical antiquity, as a reminder of those distant, heroic days. With his neo-classicism, the Revolution found its public style, a formal, restrained convention for its visual propaganda displays.

With the procession of Voltaire's bones, a change of intention came into the revolutionary ceremonies. Up to then religion had been an indispensable adjunct of public celebrations. In the Federation, which inaugurated the new epoch of national sovereignty, the Gallican Church played a central role, as it had in the coronation of the *ancien régime*. No one seriously considered any alternative. Frenchmen were not expected to take stock of their personal convictions to distinguish between the secular and religious implications of the masses and prayers that marked these great occasions. But Voltaire's burial in the Panthéon was different. It took place without benefit of clergy, with David's sophisticated showmanship eulogizing the virtues of a Rome that had flourished before Christianity was born. It was a partisan rather than a truly national ceremony. The campaign to bring the remains to Paris (they had to be taken from the abbey of Scellières because of the sale of ecclesiastical property) had been mounted by anti-clericals, and the Assembly had yielded to their pressure in exasperation at the refusal of so many of the clergy to accept the Civil Constitution. Catholics were offended, priests of the Constitutional Church led the protestations, and religious journalists did their best to pretend that the pageantry had been a farce.

Here was an example of a civic ceremony unsuited for ecclesiastical participation. Yet, with many of the faithful boycotting the State Church and anti-clericals intensifying their clamour, the question was bound to arise—on what principle does the State accept the co-operation of the Church in its public observances? In this same month of July 1791, some discourses of Mirabeau were published, revealing that the great tribune had wanted religion excluded from official ceremonies altogether. "The majestic severity of the Christian religion does not allow it to be associated with the profane spectacles, songs, dances, and sports of our national festivals." According to Talleyrand, in a report on education submitted in the last days of the Constituent Assembly, the decencies could be observed by expelling religion from joyful festivals and retaining it in sad ones—the ex-bishop had personal experience of keeping pleasure and religion in separate compartments. The Assembly did not settle the matter, but it added a unanimous rider to the Constitution, that national fêtes were needed "to preserve the memory of the French Revolution, maintain fraternity among citizens, and attach them to the Fatherland and the laws".

The Constituent Assembly had got to the point of contemplating a radical change in the position of religion in civic ceremonies. Indeed, before it finally disbanded, it had been pushed to the brink of a precipice at other tricky points along the borderline between Church and State. The ending of tithe,

the sale of ecclesiastical property and the abolition of religious congregations wrecked the vast patchwork educational system of the *ancien régime*. Decrees of December '89 and January '90 gave Departmental administrations the "surveillance of public education and of political and moral teaching", measures which took away the former powers of approbation and control of teachers exercised by bishops and *curés*. But how would new schools be organized and who would teach in them? No one knew. Amidst the anarchy, the Assembly ruled that individual monks and nuns engaged in teaching would lose half their pension if they did not carry on for the time being. Then began an uneasy search for an educational theory to fit the new national sovereignty. Some argued for liberal principles. "Everyone", said Mirabeau, "has the right to teach what he knows, and even what he does not know", a rule which he himself had often followed when speaking to the Assembly. Others wanted "patriotic schools", to produce "citizens". According to one ecclesiastical deputy (the future constitutional bishop of Quimper), liberty must yield place to moral unity, and even the influence of the family upon the child must be destroyed. Talleyrand's report of September 1791 tried to combine the liberal and the patriotic theories—no monopoly, yet a State system of education which would throw its roots down into the soul of every citizen. The report tried to maintain the balance, but there was little doubt which system was meant to prevail.

The other tract of dangerous frontier territory where the Constituent Assembly strayed was that of the *état civil*, the registration of births, marriages, and deaths. On the eve of the Revolution everyone assumed that this would always be done by the parish priest in the parish register. The rare references in the *cahiers* are simply complaints about inefficiency (there was a splendid case in Anjou of a country *curé* who neglected to keep registers for 24 years, from 1738 to 1762, so that for miles around no one had proof who was entitled to inherit anything). Under the *ancien régime* most law suits about marriage and other family matters came before the civil courts, often by the procedure known as *appel comme d'abus,* while the lawyers had established accepted ways of dove-tailing together the requirements of canon and civil law. Though the Assembly ended the "parental despotism" characteristic of the State law, this did not affect the existing working arrangements between Church and State. Insuperable difficulty did not arise until the actor, Talma, appealed to the Assembly for justice against the *curé* of Saint-Sulpice, who had refused to bless his marriage because of his profession. Durand de Maillane, the canonist, who was commissioned to look into the legal principles involved, reported that the State was concerned only with the civil contract between the two parties: the sacrament needed other dispositions, but these, and the nuptial blessing they obtained, were no affair of the legislator. The Assembly agreed that the law considered marriage only as a civil contract, but because of the outcry (a clerical journalist said town-hall marriages were "habitual fornication"), no action was taken to follow up this admission.

With the schism over the Civil Constitution of the Clergy, however, a new pressure group with unimpeachable credentials came onto the scene to reinforce the agitation of actors and radicals. Orthodox Catholics refused to go to the Constitutional clergy for their marriages. In March 1791, La Luzerne, Bishop of Langres, told his flock to resort to the provisions of the Edict of 1787, and register their marriages like Protestants. Other bishops gave similar instructions and Rome approved, provided the parties did not specifically declare themselves non-Catholics. Now that the State Church no longer had even the nominal allegiance of a majority of Frenchmen, sceptics drifting out at one end and the orthodox at the other, was it reasonable to maintain parish priests in control of the *état civil*? From the end of 1790, municipalities had been appointing *lecteurs patriotes* to perform the duty of reading official decrees, a task which the Assembly had originally attempted to impose on the *curés*. Here was a precedent. Perhaps the logical next step was to appoint lay registrars, on the analogy of the *lecteurs patriotes,* to record births, marriages, and deaths, leaving the sacraments to the priests and to the consciences of individuals.

We have seen how anti-clericalism surged forward with the meeting of the Legislative Assembly (1 October 1791), the declaration of war and the fall of the Throne (10 August 1792): how the refractory clergy came to be regarded as a fifth column in league with the enemy. Some of this suspicion rubbed off onto the constitutionals. No sooner had the Legislative met than André Chénier was suggesting winding up the Civil Constitution of the Clergy; in November, François de Neufchâteau renewed the proposal. In the following January, De Moy, the "red" *curé* of Saint-Laurent at Paris, published his notorious *Accord de la Religion et des Cultes chez une Nation Libre* proclaiming the same message with provocative embellishment—he wished to ban clerical costume, forbid clerical celibacy, and impose a civic burial service with the central liturgical theme of "sleep without hope of awakening".

In a darkening atmosphere of feverish exaltation and lurking fears, extreme courses already foreseen under the Constituent were actually adopted by the Legislative. The discussions on education were dominated by the determination not to fall back into the grip of clericalism. Condorcet still raised a voice in favour of liberalism: even the Constitution, he said, ought to be taught in State schools only as a fact, not as "a sort of political religion". But the dominant will to survive and triumph made itself felt in totalitarian proposals. In the end, on 18 August 1792, the ex-monks and nuns were forbidden to teach. The idea of patriotic indoctrination was extended from children to adults. Early in 1792 Lanthenas published an appeal for the political societies to federate together into a "universal church" with "patriotic missionaries" preaching the *"culte de la raison et de la loi"*, and on 15 April the popular societies of Paris did federate, to stage a Festival of Liberty in honour of the Swiss of the Châteauvieux Regiment and as an expiation for the shooting of republican petitioners on the Champ de Mars on 17 July 1791. David and his team devised the details, from the procession of maidens carrying the chains of the martyred Swiss mutineers to a statue of Liberty drawn by two dozen brewery horses. The *Moniteur* suggested that the festival be retained as a permanent celebration of spring-time. On the very last day of its existence, 20 September 1792, the Legislative laicized the *état civil* and legalized divorce. It was a decisive breach with the past, but the contemporary press paid little attention. In the monstrous swirl of events there were more desperate things to think about.

We have described the ceremonies and observances which expressed and propagated the dynamic enthusiasm of the Revolution. In them Catholicism had played its part, allied with the new order just as it had been allied with the old monarchy. We have seen the breakdown of this alliance. The next step, in days of exaltation and delirium, was to be the creation of a revolutionary religion, taking over the role which Catholicism had played in public life. Many of the ceremonies which the new religion was to use were there already, antedating the breach with Christianity, and surviving it. To this extent, in the famous unresolved dispute between two great historians, Mathiez is right. Aulard had argued that the religion of the Revolution was a phenomenon of the war for survival; patriotic fervour and hatred of treacherous priests were its inspirations—it was "an expedient of national defence". Mathiez replied that the revolutionary religion was there already, in essentials, at the end of the Constituent Assembly. "Far from being an artificial creation of a few men, a political expedient, a device of circumstance, it appears to us as a spontaneous creation of the French soul, late in time, but full of the flavour of eighteenth-century philosophy."

To some extent, we take sides in this quarrel according to our definition of religion. Mathiez was following Durkheim, whose view of religion limited the analysis to outward actions as social facts. But if we include in our definition—as surely, we must—some reference to personal conviction, interior promptings, mystical experience, and the operation of conscience upon conduct, a difficulty arises about the point of time at which we can properly refer to the ceremonies which expressed the enthusiasm of the Revolution as "religious".

We must recognize that the alliance between Catholicism and the movement of national regeneration in 1789 and 1790 was a reality which might have endured. Natural religion was dear to eighteenth-century publicists, but only on the lunatic fringe of journalism had there been proposals to oust the established Church. And how serious were these? Sylvain Maréchal must have known that his vision of the oldest inhabitant of the commune, "with venerable beard in place of sacerdotal ornaments", taking over from the *curé,* was as far from realization as his scheme for giving the Dauphin anatomy lessons on "the skeleton of a decapitated tyrant". Indeed, this greatest of priest-haters had his own nuptials celebrated by a constitutional clergyman in the church of Saint-Nicolas-des-Champs in April 1792; thereafter, his wife and sister-in-law regularly attended mass with his encouragement, and when he died they ensured his Christian burial. If Maréchal, "the man without God", conformed at the height of the Revolution, it is not surprising that, in 1789, even the most fanatical opponents of Christianity were unable to picture France without the traditional Gallican Church. Until the schism over the Civil Constitution hardly anyone knew how to begin to disentangle patriotic and religious ceremonies, let alone how to define separate allegiances to each. Only when it became obvious that the alliance between Catholicism and the national regeneration was collapsing, could the true revolutionary religion begin. It needed eccentrics and fanatics to give it leadership, men whose chance would never have come except in chaotic times when the crust of social conformity had broken. Even so, there was a solid base for the new venture, for it could be built upon the anti-clerical passions that sought to humiliate Catholicism and demonstrate that France could live without it, and upon the wider, almost universal conviction, inherited from the *ancien régime*, virtually uncontradicted by the *philosophes*, that no State could survive without a public religion.

On this analysis, we ought to concern ourselves rather less, in the study of the origins of the revolutionary religion, with the patriotic symbolism ante-dating the break with Catholicism, and more with the new elements (or old elements given new emphasis) which were introduced to replace the Christian contribution which was being rejected. Behind their nominal allegiance to Catholicism, the men of '89 had a core of religious belief which was sub-Christian though not consciously recognized as such, because the necessity for clarification had never been imposed. Once conventional Christian observances fell out of favour, the revolutionaries were driven to define and affirm what they really believed. Their conviction that religion is indispensable was very much a conviction of their social and political theory—but it was more than this. Mathiez, concentrating on ceremonies and reading too much into them, was passing lightly over the best arguments for his case for deep roots for the revolutionary religion. The men of '89 were full of spiritual yearnings, as well as material and political passions, and when Catholicism slipped away from them, they had a surprisingly homogeneous collective instinct about what ought to replace it. Almost to a man, they were deists, and the religion they introduced was a national, philanthropic deism. "*Adore un Dieu*", Voltaire had said in his *Poème sur la loi naturelle*, "*sois juste, et chéris ta Patrie*." From Rousseau, they took the teaching that men can communicate with God without any intermediaries, save the inspiration of the majestic fecundity and beauty of Nature. Rejecting the Christian idea of original sin, they believed in the God-given search for happiness here on earth. The State itself was founded on this basic principle of our existence. "All men", said the Declaration of Rights, "have an invincible inclination towards the search for happiness; to achieve it by their united efforts they formed into societies and established governments".

The pageantry of the revolutionary religion was not to be confined to the themes of Liberty, the Law, the Constitution, and Reason. Bounteous Nature was to be worshipped in a haze of Rousseauistic, pastoral emotion, in which solemn dedication to the fair land of France profaned by the enemy mingled with the schoolboy exuberance of men released for the day from the mephitic atmosphere of sweating assemblies. Rarely has the family, that basic institution of natural religion, been held in such ostentatious honour. Praise was heaped upon good husbands, fathers, wives, and dutiful off-spring, in terms which later generations have only dared to use in epitaphs. Old age and childhood were accorded special veneration; white-clad girls and tired old men in classical ox carts figured in all their processions. It was sincere homage, unsmilingly given, as when the National Assembly had solemnly stood to receive Jean Jacob from the Jura, 120 years of age and the oldest man in France, and the Legislative had applauded citizens who brought their children to the bar of the senate of the nation to hand in their money boxes. These men of blood, who sent their companions to the guillotine, proclaimed the religion of amity with absolute sincerity. Saint-Just's day dreams of a republican utopia included a "Temple of Friendship", where every adult must record the names of his friends every year, and explain to the magistrates why any have been removed from the list. Presumably, having sent them to the scaffold a month or two earlier would not be an acceptable reason.

It is difficult for us today to do justice to a humanitarian creed so ostentatious, and our generation, which sees agnosticism as the alternative to Christianity, cannot work up much sympathy for a brashly optimistic deism inventing portentous rituals. But the short-lived religion of the Revolution should be taken seriously. If it is, its true inspiration and origins are seen in the intellectual and literary temper of France in the second part of the eighteenth century. "The religion of the revolutionaries, which oscillates from Voltairean reason to the folly of *illuminés*", writes Trahard, "is a force of *sensibilité* rather than a dogmatic belief or an act of faith". The men of '89 had read Fénelon, Rousseau, Ossian, Richardson, Prévost, Goethe and innumerable lesser writers who dealt in this strange, almost indefinable quality of *sensibilité*, which included in its scope sentiment, emotion, susceptibility, benevolence, tenderness, sympathy, self-awareness, longing, enthusiasm, optimism—and despair. They were haunted by dreams of distant utopias and by the immediacy of the sunset; they were full of zest for life and talked of welcoming death, they analysed their emotions with sophistication, and wept like children, they sought out every refinement of argument and rhetoric, while adoring pastoral simplicity and the uncomplicated heroes of classical antiquity—and all this without relaxing for one moment their business acumen, their eye for the main chance, their desire for public office. The processions of the revolutionary religion, faintly ridiculous to anyone afterwards, were seen by them through their readings in the works of the masters of *sensibilité*, through the magic haze of pre-romanticism. To understand, we have to go back into their dream world and join them, in the quiet days before '89, in provincial academies or garret studies, on river banks, on pilgrimages to the Isle of Poplars, or like Barnave, in the paternal garden, "reading *Werther*, while the autumn wind swirled the withered leaves".

9. The Vendée and the Beginning of Terror

While the Prussians were advancing and the fate of France was in the balance—and the prison massacres were proceeding—elections to a National Convention had begun. The constitutional clergy celebrated masses at the opening of the electoral assemblies. Of the five million Frenchmen entitled to vote only one million went to the polls, but they elected representatives who were determined that the Revolution should not fail. The Convention declared that it would fight the war as a crusade. On 19 November 1792 it passed a decree that sent a shudder through the courts of Europe, an offer to help any people which wished to regain its liberty. On 15 December Cambon's decree proclaimed "war on the *châteaux*, peace for the cottages", which was an ideological way of saying that war would be paid for by plunder, in the first instance from the lands of the Church in Belgium. The King was executed on 21 January 1793: he made his last confession to a non-juring priest. Eleven days later the Republic declared war on England. In March the peasants of the Vendée rose against the Government, the beginning of a campaign of guerrilla warfare which lasted until the rule of Bonaparte. Within a few months, over half of France, a civil war within the civil war had arisen, for the revolutionaries began fighting each other. The Montagnards in the Convention defeated the Girondins by enlisting the insurrectionary forces of Paris, but the Girondins had middle-class support in the provinces, and by midsummer Marseille, Lyon, and sixty departments of the south and west were ablaze. Some bishops of the Constitutional Church were involved on the Girondin side—Philbert,

Fauchet, Lamourette, Roux. The war became more desperate, food became scarcer, and raging inflation nourished corruption and drove the poor to despair. On 2 September Paris heard the news that Toulon had surrendered to the British fleet. The Convention declared "Terror, the order of the day". And so it was for the next ten months, until July 1794 and the fall of Robespierre.

What part did religion play in the atrocious civil war that was waged in the Vendée? We must distinguish here between the motives of the rising as contemporaries saw them and as they appear today in the light of analyses of the social structure of the insurrectionary areas, and between the causes of the original outbreak and the forces which kept rebellion going once it had started, like draughts fanning a blazing torch. To their republican opponents the Vendéans were a cruel peasant rabble wearing pious images in their hats and chaplets round their necks, obeying the orders of royalist agents and fanatical churchmen. It was true enough that the rising, once started, was taken over by supporters of the *ancien régime*—nobles, or ecclesiastics like Bernier, ex-*curé* of Saint-Laud of Angers. But this was not how the insurrection had begun. About its origins there is a legend with a dual bias, for clerical historians have depicted pious peasants marching to defend their good *curés,* while anti-clerical historians have improved upon the same theme with a fable of a plot of priests who, in Michelet's words, "devised a work of art, singular and strange, a revolution against the Revolution, a republic against the Republic".

There is something (within limits) to be said for the clerical version and nothing at all for the anti-clerical one. The revolt began on the fringes of no less than five ecclesiastical dioceses—Luçon, La Rochelle, Angers, Nantes, Poitiers —and not a single bishop or ecclesiastical official made any attempt to organize resistance to the Revolution. The earliest leaders of the rioters were not priests or nobles, but an itinerant vendor of fruit and fish and a ruined *perruquier*.

True, the clergy of the heartland of the rebellion were over-whelmingly on the refractory side (though the proportion varied oddly from one locality to another: almost all re-fractories in the "Mauges" area of southern Anjou, but no less than ninety-six *curés* and five *vicaires* among the consti-tutionals, as against 134 *curés* and seventy two *vicaires* remain-ing orthodox, in the insurrectionary area of the actual depart-ment of the Vendée). Many of the clergy dispossessed by the Civil Constitution were popular with their flocks—we know that some of them were remarkably generous with their alms in hard times—while those who were not popular were at least influential, for in such an isolated rural *milieu* they were indispensible in all local business. It is clear too that the reorganization of parishes by the District authorities under the Civil Constitution legislation was bitterly resented. There were riots to preserve bells from confiscation and petitions to keep well-loved churches open. Envious clamour was raised against the intriguing "patriots" who stood well with the revolutionary officials and pulled strings to ensure that their own parishes were preserved while others were sup-pressed. Yet, all this could be said about many areas of Brittany, and Brittany remained comparatively quiet, passively accepting the revolutionary settlement of the Church. Why was the Vendée so different?

If an answer in one word is required that word is "poverty". Ever since the beginning of 1789 the peasants of the rough, infertile country of the rising had been on the verge of star-vation. They had been unfairly taxed under the *ancien régime* in comparison with other areas. Their *cahiers* had made simple requests—lower taxation, the repair of their miserable roads, and help for the infirm and indigent, who abounded. What, in fact, they received from the Revolution was a new con-solidated land tax based on the same unjust assessment, and so arranged that the cultivator had to pay it all directly, instead of some falling on the proprietor, as in the days before the reform. "In the special case of the Vendée", writes Faucheux, "there was a demoralizing impression that they were paying more out of a diminished revenue—as indeed they were". So the revolutionary government was hated. When it introduced a conscription law (Sunday 10 March was the date of enrolment) the rising began. In proportion to the population few conscripts were being called up. This made no difference. The point had been reached at which starving and disillusioned men would obey no longer. The broken nature of the country, the lack of urban rallying points for republican forces, the fact that troops were not available for quick suppressive action meant that isolated riots could combine into a full scale, wide-spread rebellion, and once it had begun those who had committed themselves were doomed if they surrendered.

But the Vendéan rising was more than an attack upon a hated government: it was also an attack upon a specific social class which was identified with the revolutionary régime —the bourgeoisie of the country towns, the officials, and the richer farmers. These were the men with capital who had bought the lion's share of ecclesiastical property when it came onto the market. Earlier historians had noticed the division between town and country and the peasants' envious hatred of the acquirers of the *biens nationaux,* but the study of these social tensions upon a detailed statistical and geographical basis is a recent development, inspired by Paul Bois' *Paysans de l'Ouest* (1960). Bois' problem was to explain the motives of the *chouans,* the catholic-royalist brigands of the Sarthe, to the north of the main Vendéan war zone. In 1789 the peasants of the west of the Sarthe had been more hostile to nobles and clergy than their fellows in the rest of the department, yet from 1793 they furnished the recruits for a sinister guerrilla feud against the revolutionary bourgeoisie. The paradox is explained once the destination of the *biens nationaux* is analysed. In most of the department there was little ecclesiastical property for sale, and the peasants were too poor to buy it; in the west, there was more property for sale and the peasants were prosperous enough to have obtained it— had not the bourgeoisie outbid them at the auctions. A similar analysis, more straightforward in this case, has been made of

the areas of the Vendéan rising by Charles Tilly and later by
Marcel Faucheux. In the District of Sables d'Olonne, for
example, out of 217 buyers of *biens nationaux,* only fifty-
seven were small peasants or artisans; in the District of Cholet
only 156 out of a total of 640. Those who were able to buy
ecclesiastical property, one might conclude, became enthusiasts
for the Revolution, which was their guarantee that they could
keep it: those who were defeated at the auctions became
acutely conscious of the religious loyalties which reinforced
their hatred of their richer and victorious rivals.

That there is a sociological explanation for the role played
by religion in the Vendéan rising does not mean that the
religious motivation has been explained away. Collectively
and statistically these obscure, grim fighters can be added
together in groups acting in patterns which explain, in retrospect, why they were the ones to rebel, while other peasants
with similar religious convictions did not carry their dis-
satisfaction to the point of civil war. But, taken individually,
there is little doubt what their inspiration in battle will be,
for the forefront of men's minds is filled by their most avow-
able motives. In their own eyes the "Whites" who lay in
ambush for the "Blues" along the sunken lanes and dense
hedgerows of the Bocage, and who were shot and guillotined
in droves by republican military commissioners, were fighting
for their families, for the Virgin and the saints, for their own
local ideal of "liberty"—liberty to contract out of the nation's
unjust wars and taxation, and to stay at home and hear mass
said by their old familiar priests.

The religious inspiration of the rebels confirmed the worst
suspicions of republicans. The non-juring clergy of France
were in league with the enemy, "lighting torches of fanaticism
and civil war" behind the battle lines, while their *confrères*
in the Emigration encouraged the onslaught of the despots.
Against this background of foreign and civil war the strange
phenomenon of "de-Christianization" arose. It had been fore-
shadowed in August–September 1792 when a beginning was
made of persecuting the orthodox clergy and of undermining

the unhappy Constitutional Church—in the deportation laws, the September massacres, and the laicization of the *état civil*. Thereafter religious ceremonies at Paris began to come under official disapproval. The Commune tried to ban the midnight mass of Christmas, and the Convention refrained from sending a deputation to the Corpus Christi procession of June '93, though it suspended its session to allow representatives to attend as individuals. Four months later, when Terror had been declared the "order of the day", a permanent institution until the enemy was defeated, the attack on Catholicism reached a new intensity, qualitatively as well as quantitatively different from what had gone before. Priests were compelled to abjure their vocation; there was sacrilegious masquerading, vandalism, and destruction in churches; a new calendar was enforced, which got rid of Sundays and Saints' days. In the end a revolutionary religion was introduced to serve the moral ends of the nation in place of discredited Catholicism.

In an attempt to understand this vast, chaotic overturn, the following chapters will trace separately three of its major aspects: the campaign to eradicate Christianity, the foundation of the new revolutionary religion, and the fate of the clergy at the hands of terrorists and de-Christianizers. An analysis of this kind is dangerous, since it produces an explanation of men's actions at the expense of making their motives too clear-cut, too single-minded. So we must remember that all these things were happening confusedly together in the short space of nine months of crisis and panic, in which men were dreaming of a far-distant future as they fought for day-to-day survival. In an account of what happened under the Terror the historian must always leave a wide margin for irrationality. The explanation of certain broad tendencies in the pattern of events may be obvious, but the explanation of the peculiar actions of individuals—the terrorists, the de-Christianizers, the persecuted clergy—within those broad tendencies, leads into obscure byways running off over the edge of the map of rationality.

10. De-Christianization

De-Christianization was not an invention of the central Government. The movement had begun in the provinces before the Convention passed the legislation changing the calendar (7 October 1793), and a great deal had happened before Barère, on 6 November, obtained the decree authorizing communes to suppress religious observances if they wished to do so. It is true that the new calendar, and the complacency with which the Convention received deputations of clerics renouncing their ministry, was sensational proof that the government regarded revolutionary France as a post-Christian country. But, by and large, the Convention connived at de-Christianization, rather than encouraged it. This was true also of the Committee of Public Safety, acting collectively. On 27 October 1793 it censured one of the *représentants en mission* for excessive severities towards Catholics. "You must not give them an opportunity to say that the liberty of religious practice is being violated and that war is being waged against religion itself. Seditious and unpatriotic priests must be punished, but the title of priest as such must not be proscribed." Robespierre opposed the de-Christianization from the start. He fastidiously rejected the demonstrators who fooled around in copes and chasubles and, as a statesmen, he saw that their antics were providing propaganda for foreign enemies. Danton, for different reasons (he was trying to slow down the Terror), came out on Robespierre's side. Even the Commune of Paris, which became a directing agent for de-Christianization in the capital, was reluctant to join in at first; the proposal of 8 November, to hold a procession in ridicule of ecclesiastical "bagatelles", was rejected as unsuited to the "dignity of the magistrates of the people".

In Paris, the politicians who actively promoted the de-Christianization were adventurers on the margins of power—exhibitionists who sought to bring themselves to notice or intriguers who wished to divert attention from their own misdemeanours. Among the former class was Chaumette, a Rousseauistic dreamer, vain and homosexual, as proud of his position as *procureur* of the Commune (he noted in his diary) as Louis XIV had been in all his splendour; there were too, the members of the extremist *Comité central des sociétés populaires*, Proly, the illegitimate son of Kaunitz, the Austrian statesman, Pereira, a Portuguese Jew, and Cloots, a German baron and "the personal enemy of God". In their wake into the movement came Hébert, that crudely witty, idealistic journalist, caught up in the imaginary identity of his creation, Père Duchesne, an extremist by self-hallucination. The intriguers were the *"Pourris"*, understrappers of Danton, deep in financial scandals, Thuriot, Fabre, and Chabot, the ex-Capuchin. They were creating a furore to stave off enquiry into their peculations or, perhaps, as Louis Jacob, Fabre's biographer says, to "get back into power to save their skins". Robespierre, with his flair for detecting corruption, was hot on their trail, ready to denounce "their indulgence for aristocracy and tyranny" under cover of "the war they have declared against the divinity".

Yet, while Robespierre may be accepted as an authority on the motives of the *pourris*, this does not mean that he was right in dismissing the de-Christianization as their conspiratorial invention. Though in the end Paris set the pace for the movement, the original impulse came from some of the *représentants en mission* in the provinces. The first to act was Fouché at Nevers, assisted by Chaumette, who was visiting his home town at the time. On 22 September a Feast of Brutus was held in the Church of Saint-Cyr, Fouché preached a sermon against "religious sophistry", and afterwards presided over a ceremony in honour of married love. Three days later, he denounced ecclesiastical celibacy and ordered unmarried priests to adopt a child or an old person. On 10 October his notorious decree was published; the French people recognized no religion but that of morality, no dogma but that of its own sovereignty, and the dead were to be buried in a civic cemetery, with the bleak inscription at the gates, "Death is an eternal sleep". Meanwhile, on 1 October, André Dumont at Abbeville compelled two constitutional priests to renounce their ministry; by the end of the month he was carrying on his campaign against the "imposters", "harlequins", and "black beasts" at Amiens. On 7 October, the representative Rühl held a ceremony at Reims for smashing the flask of holy oil used at the coronation. Brought down from heaven by a dove at the prayer of St Rémi for the consecration of Clovis, it ended its career thirteen centuries later under the hammer of the local blacksmith. Other representatives emulated these achievements—Albitte, Dartigoeyte, Hentz and Bô, Milhaud and Guyardin, Faure, Delacroix, Laplanche, Laignelot, Mallarmé, Javogues, Châles, Carrier, Isabeau and Tallien, Vadier, Collot. Wherever the de-Christianization was ruthlessly pressed on—as it was in the departments of the Nièvre, the Loiret, the Allier, the Bas-Rhin, the Loire, the Nord, the Morbihan, the Haute-Garonne, the Gironde, the Ariège, and the Isère—the impulse came from one of these fanatical proconsuls. They were desperate men following desperate courses in the chaos of a war for survival. Their de-Christianization policies were partly the reflection of their own hatred of the Catholicism which had betrayed the Revolution, and partly an expedient to bolster morale and whip up frenzy among the members of the clubs and the officials and all those other Frenchmen who were committed, however vaguely, to the Revolution. Like the execution of the King, sacrilege was to be a gesture of defiance, a symbol of the determination to destroy the old world, a deliberate decision to press on beyond the point of no return, a final commitment to the oath to "live free or die'.

Of the de-Christianizers among the *représentants en mission,* Fouché was an ex-Oratorian, Laplanche an ex-Benedictine, and Châles an ex-canon of Chartres. Former ecclesiastics indeed figure prominently in the chronicles of local sacrilege.

Two Doctrinaires of the *collège* assisted Laplanche at Bourges, and when the revolutionary committee there decided to send "apostles of reason" round the countryside some of the volunteers for the mission were priests who had unfrocked themselves. The chief de-Christianizer at Havre, an anti-clerical tailor, was accompanied on his visitations by an ex-*vicaire,* who "sang a blasphemous song of his own composing". Almost everywhere ambiguous figures of this kind are found, renegade monks and priests bent on demonstrating their hatred for the vocation they had abandoned. To a degree the explanation of the phenomenon may be prosaic: it takes all sorts to make a good bout of de-Christianization, and on the principle of "man bites dog" these startling reversals of allegiance would always be reported—our evidence may be overweighted. Yet there are instances enough to oblige us to speculate further. Family pressures sometimes pushed men into ecclesiastical careers under the *ancien régime*; maybe they were now taking their revenge upon an unwanted vocation. Perhaps their renunciation of the past would be suspect and their place in the new order insecure unless they went to untoward extremes. Their hatred of religion was, maybe, something of a mask. According to Madelin's interpretation Fouché voted the death of the King because he saw the moderates were cowards, and then went on coldly and relentlessly to play the part of a terrorist—though this, surely, can only be part of the truth. These men, over-familiar with ceremonies, no doubt adopted the gestures of de-Christianization with interior reservations—like Guillaume Imbert of Limoges, who threw the skull of St Martial into the corner of the sacristy, then went back at night to rescue the relic and preserve it. Maybe for some the decision to abandon a religious vocation had been, in itself, such a psychological crisis that it made apostasy easy—"no crime can haunt him now", said La Harpe of such a one, "for he began with the greatest crime of all".

These are hard words, but nobody cares for renegades. Historians, clerical and anti-clerical alike, tend to sit in the seat of the scornful when they have to do with turncoats, more especially turncoats who helped to smash up archaeological remains and piled documentary evidence onto bonfires. Yet the proconsuls of the Terror and their assistants must be judged more by the emergencies they faced and the sort of leadership that their followers required of them than by the contrast between their actions and their antecedents. And when the full story of the *curés rouges* and the *sans-culotte* monks is written more true idealists may be found in their ranks than has been imagined—men whose former religious vocation had left them with a dream of an egalitarian, regenerated society arising from the Terror. Since the early days of the Revolution clerical voices had been raised asking for the final instalment of reform, the decisive step into true equality; pamphlets had been published by the *abbé* Cournaud, the *abbé* Fauchet (later a Constitutional bishop), and *curé* Dolivier of Étampes, while other parish priests wrote egalitarian essays in the *Feuille Villageoise*. This demand was put in grim terms of class warfare by a *curé* of Auvergne in a brochure of 1790, addressed to the bourgeois "third estate" on behalf of "the people and artisans". "Don't deceive yourselves. In throwing stones, burning *châteaux,* or murdering nobles, we weren't meaning just to minister to your vanity . . . Either come down to our level or lift us up to yours. Choose!" About this time, Jacques Roux, *curé* of Saint-Thomas-de-Carnac, had to flee to Paris because his parishioners took him at his word when he preached that the land belonged to all. By 1793 he had become one of the chief publicists of the extreme social left, an *enragé,* denouncing hoarders and speculators and teaching that "true religion consists in the love of one's fellows"—until the Convention, always solicitous about property, had him arrested in September. Two of the clerical *représentants en mission,* both ex-Oratorians, attempted to put these egalitarian ideas into practice, basing their emergency decrees upon the principle of equality of sacrifice. One, mysteriously, was Fouché, into whose hard complex mind sentimental communism entered as a brief wartime madness.

The other was Joseph Lebon whose ruthless administration saved Cambrai from the enemy. "If, when the Revolution is over", he said, "we still have the poor with us, our revolutionary toils will have been in vain". In the days of the Thermidorian reaction he seemed doubly sinister as a terrorist, for he had made arrangements at Arras to give émigré property to the poor. At his trial Lebon claimed that there had been a continuity between his life as an Oratorian and his work as a terrorist—"I derived most of my revolutionary maxims from the Gospels which, from beginning to end, preach against the rich and against priests". The renegade clergy of France deserve a greater place in the history of socialism than the very modest niche so far allowed to them.

Lebon was only a moderate de-Christianizer. He detested priests, and tried to force them to marry by the threat of conscription, but he did not close churches and he tried to ensure that clerical pensions were paid. Perhaps the ultimate explanation of his mingled harshness and sympathy is found in his private life—his mother's insanity, brought on he believed, by the fulminations of the orthodox clergy, and his brief, idyllic marriage to his cousin, Elisabeth Régnier. Fouché, another foe of clerical celibacy, had found happiness in marriage, a fact which he proclaimed in ludicrous ceremonies at Nevers. The passionate allegiance of some of these ex-ecclesiastics to the Revolution, and certain excesses of the de-Christianization polices were conditioned by their feelings of sexual release and their gratitude for domestic felicity.

There is a great deal we still need to know to understand the renegade churchmen who threw in their lot with the Revolution. Many left little impression on the record, as they were essentially educators or administrators—presidents of District assemblies, bureaucrats, committee men; in some rural areas there was no one literate to replace them. A few were inspired by a dream of egalitarian regeneration, a few more terrorists, a few de-Christianizers, a few in due course supported the revolutionary religion. Some did more than

one of these things, and we would learn much about revolutionary France and about human nature if some researcher
could locate and describe them in their categories, telling us
which categories overlapped most and which predominated.

Je suis leur chef, il faut que je les suive. In the de-
Christianization, the *représentants en mission* were leading
by ordering actions which their followers consciously or subconsciously desired. Frenchmen wanted to lash out at the
émigré priests behind the invaders, the Catholic Vendéans
who were stabbing the fatherland from behind, the treacherous
orthodox clergy, the constitutionals suspect of moderantism
and federalism. It was easy to see how popular anti-clericalism,
full of memories of the scandals of the *ancien régime,* and
inflamed by pamphleteers and the revolutionary theatre, might
erupt in some vivid, symbolic demonstrations against the
Church. In Paris, and in some other large towns, this is
roughly what happened. Obvious targets for buffoonery and
destruction existed, together with patriotic reasons for attack-
ing them, and the police were prepared to smile tolerantly.
This is the picture of how de-Christianization broke out in
the capital as given by Mercier, author of the *Tableau de Paris*
and a journalist of genius. It was an affair of the lower
orders, of the dregs of the people. They had appeared to
believe in the mass, but beneath their conformism had lurked
hostility and scepticism. Thus the splendid structure of
Catholicism had been like a tree blasted by lightning, intact to
all appearances, but ready to crumble to powder at a touch.
Casting off their superficial respect for religion, and intoxi-
cated by the idea that they were now sovereign, the people
took the opportunity for debauch, destruction, and plunder.
There were naked dancers and drunken children in the ruined
churches and among the gravestones; presidents of revolutionary tribunals wore emeralds from monstrances in their rings,
and men of the sections had shirts made from choirboys'
surplices; the second-hand shops displayed chasubles among
pantalons and syringes, and lavatory seats alongside altar
frontals. Behind the plunder and destruction there was no

aim, no conviction; the people were acting, not out of "fanaticism", but "with a derision, an irony, a saturnalian gaiety that astonished all beholders".

What Mercier says about Paris does not necessarily apply to the rest of the country, and certainly not to rural France. One must remember too that he was writing his reminiscences at a time when "the dregs of the people" were blamed for everything outrageous in the Revolution. Only rarely did the scenes of de-Christianization come up to Mercier's bacchanalian standards. Village atheists drinking from the ciborium and challenging God to use his thunderbolts, and committee men hauling down "exterior signs of the cult" in accordance with the law, were sometimes acting with reasonable sobriety, providing a theatrical demonstration of the patriotic case for simple people—keeping "a school of demystification", in Richard Cobb's phrase. Sometimes, the destruction, far from being enlivened with free drink and naked dancers, was just a boring "working-bee". Towards the end of 1793, breaking up churches was a less scandalous occupation than it would have seemed three years earlier. Since the reorganization of parishes and the sale of church property, legitimate demolitions had been proceeding, often to make way for municipal improvements. Then came the demands of war. Bells, grilles, and railings were dragged away to be melted down for armaments. "A sanctuary can do without a grille", said the popular society of Saint-Florentin (about the abbey of Pontigny), "but the defence of the Fatherland cannot do without pikes". Some silverware had been handed in to the Mint in the early days of the Revolution; what remained was confiscated at the time of *la patrie en danger*. Church buildings were taken over for military use as ration stores, prisons, saltpetre factories. Chappe's visual telegraph to the battlefront accounted for the decapitation of the spire of Notre-Dame de l'Epine at Châlons. Churches were full of tombs of aristocrats, armorial bearings, crowns, fleurs-de-lys; the removal of these symbols of feudalism and tyranny provided dress rehearsals for the ravages of de-Christianization. In May 1793 the spire of the Sainte Chapelle was demolished because scaffolding to remove the crown from the summit would have been too expensive; early in August the royal tombs in the abbey of Saint-Denis were violated. Meanwhile, ever since 1790, the bureaucrats of Departments, Districts, and municipalities had been finding offices in empty monasteries, and the manifold clubs of the Revolution had moved into redundant churches, where the saints in their niches were a standing invitation for adoption by caps of liberty, or for demolition to make way for a plaster Brutus or Marat. The sale of church property, the political and ecclesiastical reorganization of France, and the war would have accounted for some of the revolutionary vandalism, even if there had been no recognizable de-Christianization movement.

In provincial France, the picture of the de-Christianization which we can form at present is so complex as almost to defy generalization. In some places, more especially in villages, a lead is given by a few enthusiasts; at Noyon, it is an official, the *procureur-syndic* of the District; at Aix-en-Provence, the *comité de surveillance* directs everything (it boasted to the Convention of the "cross of silvered wood which we are using at the moment as a broom handle"). At Beauvais, it is the club encouraged by a visit from the *armée révolutionaire,* which arranges an orderly programme of de-Christianization, ending with a procession to the church of Saint-Pierre to smash up the confessionals. Everything was neatly organized; coats of arms, weather cocks, emblems, organs were demolished by qualified carpenters, masons, and other tradesmen, duly paid by the authorities. Clearly there were inspirational de-Christianizations and official ones. One day, when the chronological and geographical incidence, along with the intensity, of the movement, have been exhaustively studied, a pattern, such as Georges Lefebvre has detected in the *Grande Peur,* may appear. There will be numerous "original" centres, probably of two contrasting types, the one in strongly anti-clerical areas where people broke out to do what for a long time they had felt like doing, and the other in areas where riots against the removal of the church bells or the enforcement of the *décadi* provoked the authorities to counter measures. From these centres, the news will travel, and will give rise to imitations elsewhere. Some of the main channels of communication are obvious. *Représentants en mission* sent their reports and, sometimes, their spoils to the Convention, and the Parisian press relayed the news out again to the armies and the departments. Troops moving to the battle-fronts described the latest fashion and gave a hand in enforcing it. Clubs of the towns sent out "apostles" or less dramatically named agents round the countryside. Committee men moved between towns and local administrators corresponded. Details of the Festival of Reason in Paris were first heard of in Bordeaux when a letter from one enthusiast to another was read in the club. At Violès (Vaucluse) no one knew how to celebrate the *décadi* until a de-Christianizer from Orange told them the importance of having a "goddess on the altar". Affairs in Beauvais were hastened on by the visit of a deputation of revolutionary women from Paris, a more formidable sort of liaison.

The provincial de-Christianization, says Richard Cobb (whose studies of the revolutionary mentality and the complexities of local circumstance are transforming our understanding of the Revolution), was "popular, authoritarian, and military". It was popular in the sense that the "active, vocal minority" which pursued it was proceeding by direct, theatrical action; this action was necessarily authoritarian and military, because the majority in rural France would not accept the de-Christianization except under threat of force. The chief agencies of this force were the troops of the line, whether called in by a *représentant en mission* or incidently, as they moved to the battle fronts, and the "revolutionary armies", the *sans-culotte* militias that toured the countryside enforcing the revolutionary decrees, especially those against food hoarders. Parisian battalions of this *sans-culotte* force went out to the District of Pontoise to suppress riots against the confiscation of the bells, to Auxerre to secure an area vital to the food supplies of the capital, and to rebellious Lyon. Expeditions left Toulouse to stop the observance of Sunday at Grenade, and Valence to harass villages that were agitating for the reopening of churches. Apart from such major "military" excursions detachments also went on tour, sometimes brutally, as in the Morbihan and the Bas-Rhin, though more often with much noise and little violence to persons. Anti-clerical, imbued with the townsman's suspicion of country folk, enraged against food hoarders, fearful of the hostile peasants all around, and inspired not infrequently by drink and inflammatory discussion in taverns, they undertook the more superficial chores of the de-Christianization with anarchical enthusiasm. Often, they devastated the church furniture and passed on without effect; sometimes, they inspired local anti-clericals to action which continued after they had departed. Only in departments where determined de-Christianizing *représentants en mission* were in charge did the revolutionary armies try to force the clergy to abdicate and to marry, set up temples of Reason, and push the de-Christianization through to a bitter, logical conclusion.

The acceptance of the de-Christianization idea and the way in which it was executed would depend, of course, upon a whole variety of local circumstances. In one of the original centres, the tiny commune of Ris-Orangis (which influenced the surrounding Corbeil area), all the inhabitants seemed to care about was to avoid paying out money; they deposed the *curé* and said that those who wanted to add anything to the "primitive religion" of humanity (no buildings to maintain) would have to do so at their own expense. The people of the hamlet of Mennecy (Seine-et-Oise), who declared their church closed, in defiance of the District authorities, claimed they were abandoning Christianity because their *curé* lived in concubinage. In many places, the attack on the Church was an aspect of the hatred between town and country, as the activities of the "revolutionary armies" indicate. Sometimes it was a question of rich versus poor, big farmers backing the *curé,* and the agricultural labourers against him. At Bourges, Laplanche made the rich pay for the repair of the cathedral, since they alone were on the side of the priests. In a few areas, Protestants took revenge for the persecutions they had undergone, in others, orthodox Catholics were not entirely averse to seeing the constitutional *curé* subjected to vexations. Once the spark had taken hold, the fire could feed on any fuel—local traditions and rivalries, personal feuds, eccentricities and fancies, fear of defeat or confidence in victory, hatred of the past or hope for the future. And there would be no lack of willing helpers. Here was a patriotic activity within the powers of the meanest citizen, in which indeed street urchins, ne'er-do-wells, drunks, and village idiots had special functions to perform.

11. Reason and the Être Suprême

On 13 July 1793 Marat was assassinated. There was a spontaneous demand from the people for a patriotic funeral. The first completely lay ceremony of the Revolution had been the translation of Voltaire's remains to the Panthéon; since then, in January 1793, Paris had paid its last homage (organized by David) to Le Peletier, stabbed by a royalist, and in April to Lazowski, a member of the Commune, poisoned, so it was said, by aristocrats. Then came the obsequies of Marat. On 15 July his embalmed body lay in republican state in the chapel of the Cordeliers—no longer a chapel, of course, but an annexe of the Club. The crowds filing past were shown the bath in which the tribune of the people had expired, and his blood-stained shirt; simple folk gaped at the books of the old convent library, stacked high in the side-chapels, and wondered at the indefatigable industry of the murdered journalist who had written so many volumes. On the following day the Convention and Sections joined in a funeral procession, and at midnight the body was placed in its tomb in the Cordelier's garden—a cave in a mound of granite rocks, surmounted by a pyramid, with an inscription to "the friend of the people". On 17 July the women of a revolutionary society took an oath to bring up their children in the cult of Marat and to give them no other Scripture but his works. A day later was celebrated the feast of the translation of the heart of Marat to the Cordelier's club room, where it was suspended in an urn from the roof, amidst applause. The Revolution was accumulating saints for its calendar.

Rather less than a month later, on 10 August, the anniversary of the fall of the Throne, David organized another ceremony, this time for the acceptance of the new Constitution (which had not yet been submitted to the nation and which never went into force). The centre-piece was a dramatic new invention, a colossal statue of the Goddess Nature, spurting water from her breasts into an ornamental pool, on the site of the Bastille. Here, Hérault de Séchelles, a *ci-devant* courtier and magistrate of the Parlement of Paris, and now a member of the Committee of Public Safety, gave a speech of invocation as he drank of the fountain—"Sovereign of nations, savage or civilized—O Nature!—this great people is worthy of thee. It is free. After traversing so many centuries of errors and servitudes, it had to return to the simplicity of thy ways to rediscover liberty and equality". Aristocratic and atheistic, the orator had limited himself to an austere, philosophic minimum. But given more content, moral force, and enthusiasm, the concept of Nature might serve as a beginning for a patriotic, official religion; at least, it was here being used to replace the Christian element in a national ceremony. And the storm of de-Christianization was about to break, creating a void which the new cult might fill.

The revolutionary calendar (7 October) added little to Hérault de Séchelles' vague pantheism. Its months (by the nomenclature introduced on 24 November) evoked the cycles of the weather and the seasons; its days were diversified by a "botanical lyricism"—shades of Jean-Jacques and of the country life that had become the civilized idea of happiness in the last few years before the Revolution, and of the vain yearning to escape from the fetid streets of Paris where the business of liberty was being transacted. Romantic details apart, the main impact of the calendar was probably that of an instrument of de-Christianization. The logical pursuit of the decimal system was taken to be more important than Sunday; the world began anew, not with the birth of Jesus, but with the proclamation of a republic in France. The craft of priests who had synchronized Church festivals with the cycle of nature, was now circumvented; in future, the harvest would be garnered without bonfires to St John, the grey skies of winter would cease to make men tremble for the souls of the departed, and coquettes would parade in the sunshine while the Fête-Dieu went unheeded.

Though the new calendar was a sensational gesture, the idea of separating the new generation from memories of the past had been active in the Revolution for some time already. Enthusiasts, avoiding saints' names for their children, had resorted to heroes like Brutus or Cato, or to new inventions incorporating "Liberty" or "Federation". Since the spring of 1791, when there had been a campaign to get the quai des Théatins named after Voltaire, some street names had been changed, and from August 1793 there was a rush of innovation, eliminating everything that smacked of feudalism or religion. Even the idea of compiling a laicized calendar was not new. It had been a sort of parlour game in the seventies and eighties, and Sylvain Maréchal, the atheist, had raised a scandal in 1788 with his *Almanach des honnêtes gens,* a calendar for "the first year of Reason". He had given Jesus two days, the same as Rousseau, Epicurus, Helvétius, Michel Angelo, Marcus Aurelius, and Socrates, and he had left 15 August blank, his own birthday and, as it happens, Napoleon's. In January 1793 Maréchal produced a new, republican version of his almanac, which delighted Chaumette—"we will replace St Antony and his pig by the festivals of Solon, Lycurgus, and Brutus". It was offered to the Convention, but was passed over in favour of something less flamboyant, though equally divorced from Christian tradition.

Though the new calendar did not sketch out a liturgy for a revolutionary religion, it did establish the *décadi* in place of Sunday—a standing invitation for the inventors of new observances. The great day of triumph for the de-Christianizers in Paris, when the Convention received the treasures Fouché had sent from the churches of the Nièvre and heard Gobel, Metropolitan of Paris, renounce his functions, provided the inventors with their opportunity. That evening, the Department and Commune decided that the next *décadi* (10 November: 20 brumaire) would be celebrated with a festival of Reason in the cathedral of Notre-Dame. It was windy and

rainy on the day; the ceremonies were ragged and their para-
phernalia shop-soiled. The Convention did not attend the first
performance, but a visit from the demonstrators persuaded
half the representatives to go for an encore. Because it was
so hastily devised, the shabby scenario of the new cult was
revealing in its naivety. The cathedral became the Temple of
"Reason"; inside was a "Mountain", with a Temple of
"Philosophy" at the summit, from which emerged a goddess
of "Liberty". The ideological content was rudimentary. It
was the minimum required for a patriotic, Jacobin, anti-
clerical substitute for Christianity.

The example of Paris was widely imitated: indeed it had
been anticipated. On the previous *décadi* at Clermont there
had been a festival with a "goddess", and a month earlier, at
Havre, the publication of the revolutionary calendar had been
welcomed with a *fête décadaire* in honour of Reason. These
were the sort of gestures for which the times were calling. In
some places, the celebrations were essentially a formalization
of the de-Christianization, with solemn bonfires of vestments
and confessionals. Amiens, with a goddess of dubious morals,
is such a case; so too is Poitiers, where a dozen priests were
compelled to make humiliating abdications, and revolutionaries
with whips chased a masquerade of sorcerers, popes, monks,
angels, and kings through the church of Saint-Porchaire. In a
very few places atheism was the keynote of the festival, as at
Rochefort under the representative Lequinio. But most of the
ceremonies of Reason were deist in inspiration. "Reason" was
not always emphasized; quite often, the "Law", "Truth",
"Liberty" or "Nature" took its place. At Beauvais there were
three goddesses, Reason, Liberty, and Equality, and worship
was paid to "the Being who made us all equal". Where Reason
was the theme of the festival it was taken as an emanation
from the Divinity, a challenge to the masquerades of priests
who concealed God from the eyes of mankind. "What is the
cult of Reason, if not the homage we render to the order
established by the eternal wisdom", was the formula at Auch.
"Reason is God's noblest gift", was the proclamation at

Chartres. In keeping with these sentiments, the goddesses were usually girls of good family and morals, and the hymns and discourses breathed a Rousseauistic yearning to know God without intermediaries. Virtuous men were praised and, in some festivals, reverence was paid to an unecclesiastical Jesus, "whose only possessions were his virtues, and whose only crown was of thorns". Salaville, a *philosophe* and an atheist, published a gloomy article complaining of the personification of the "*Étre Suprême*" in the observances of the cult of Reason, instead of leaving this term to stand for nothing more than a convenient presupposition at the end of the chain of cause and effect; Frenchmen were "trying to be republicans in time, but royalists in eternity".

Salaville was out of touch with his generation. If the grotesque excesses of de-Christianization were ended, what would remain of the new national cult? Not a cold, sceptical Reason, but a warm, naive, moralizing, patriotic deism. Robespierre and the revolutionary *dirigeants* destroyed the professional de-Christianizers, whose ambitions were threatening the dictatorship, and whose crude policies were alienating the countryside and degrading the Republic in the eyes of Europe. After this it was in the logic of events that the cult of Reason, purged of its more blatant anti-clerical manifestations, should become the cult of the *Être Suprême*. On 6 April 1794 Couthon, in the name of the Committee of Public Safety, announced "a project of a *fête décadaire* dedicated to the Eternal", and on 7 May Robespierre laid down the creed of the new religion: the existence of the Supreme Being and the immortality of the soul. This time, the preparations for the festival were unhurried, and David excelled himself. The chosen day, 20 prairial (8 June) was not only a *décadi,* it was Whit-Sunday: the Republic was to vie with one of the great days of the Church. All was done in good taste, in the mode of classical antiquity, so that the fastidious Robespierre himself could lead the procession in his blue coat, bearing a bouquet of berries, grain, and flowers. "*Voyez ce bourgre-là,* he is not satisfied with being the boss, he wants to be God as well!'' In its direct context the gibe was unjust; in a wider application it contained an envenomed truth, for Robespierre's crime lay in that self-conscious rectitude which allowed him to usurp the justice of God, and to use the guillotine as an instrument of moral regeneration.

The Convention had decreed the observance of the feast of the *Être Suprême* throughout France, but had not said who was to organize it. Generally the municipalities and popular societies obliged. Except at Nevers and Havre, the adherents of Reason seemed to have made no objection to transferring to the new official observances. Now that there was no de-Christianization to enliven proceedings the ceremonies tended to attract the more respectable citizens and to be boring to the others. The popular society of Beauvais was relieved to get rid of some of the old agitators—"we have expelled from our midst all those individuals whose morality did not conform to the principles of republicanism". The "props" of Reason were easily adapted for the liturgy of the Supreme Being. At Brest, Prieur (de la Marne) ordered the "Mountain of Reason" to be "repaired and touched up". At Besançon, citizeness Cussy, who had played the Goddess of Reason, processed again in a less Olympian role, three old men and some fruits of the earth being added to her waggon to make it respectable. Some communes decided not to stage another festival, but simply paid the local plasterer or painter to obliterate the inscription "Temple of Reason" and replace it with "The French people recognizes the Supreme Being and the immortality of the soul". Perhaps, if official encouragement had been extended over a longer period, greater enthusiasm might have been generated. As it was, fifty days after the festival of 20 prairial, Robespierre went to the scaffold.

Some day the progress of research will enable us to generalize about the impact of the de-Christianization and the revolutionary cults in different areas and among varying strata of the population. Aulard claimed that the cult of Reason was most successful in ardently Catholic districts, or in those where there was danger from the foreign invader or

internal rebels; this supported his argument that the revolutionary religion was "an expedient of national defence".
But as we have seen, many other factors were operating, not
the least being whims of fanatical individuals. Statistics of
"republican" first names as against Christian names show
startling differences between localities. At Poitiers, out of
593 births in Year II, only sixty-two children were given
republican names alone—mostly orphans or the children of
officials; at Beauvais, out of 376 names, as many as 178 were
republican. In two-thirds of the communes, of the Loir-et-
Cher, the names are exclusively Christian, yet in some of the
other communes most names are republican. There were
differing degrees of "republicanism" in the names chosen.
Derivatives from flowers or virtues were simply non-Christian.
Extremists preferred "Marat" and "Peletier", and among the
sans-culottes of Paris (or rather, among their wives), Brutus,
Marat, and Peletier became a sort of trinity of revolutionary
saints, spoken of with quasi-religious adoration. When a map
of France and a table of social classes showing the incidence
of republican names is compiled, special weight will have to
be given to the occurrence of these three "martyrs of liberty".

Représentants en mission were strict in enforcing the *décadi*.
This was recognized as the point at which the battle with
Christianity could prove decisive. By the decree of 14–16
frimaire, citizens were to assemble to hear the laws proclaimed
and efforts were made to sweeten this statutory attendance
with music, gymnastics, and other embellishments. One
Poupinel, a writer of republican hymns who accompanied the
representative on his tours, laid down the policy for Falaise
in a letter to the popular society there. "Let us put the *décadi*
in place of Sunday", he said, "without actually destroying
the latter; let us use civic pomp to make people forget the old
displays of superstition; in a word, provide more striking and
attractive alternatives to the ceremonies that for so long have
deceived the people, and the skeleton of sacerdotalism will
disintegrate of its own accord".

Since citizens were determined to marry and could not help being born and dying, there were ample opportunities for devising "occasional offices", "civic sacraments" for the republican cult. Enthusiasts who had no interesting events in their families to provide one of these opportunities for patriotic zeal could always have a republican renewal of their marriage at the *autel de la patrie* or at the foot of the Mountain, or (a supreme testimony of fanaticism) they could arrange for a "de-baptization". When the cult of the Être Suprême died away after the fall of Robespierre, the *décadi* and the civic sacraments continued, drab and uninspiring. The de-Christianization had formulated and compacted anticlericalism as an "interest" in French life, bound up with the destiny of the Revolution; it had also broken down the lethargical mystique of popular conformity which had made the Church appear so all-embracing and powerful under the *ancien régime*. But to birth and marriage the revolutionary cults brought no magic, for death no consolation. Christian conformity, perhaps, has the effect of innoculating a people against deism, leaving agnosticism or atheism (failing a reform of Christianity itself) as the only alternatives. This is what Mercier thought when he heard the errand boy say that "there wasn't a God any more, only Robespierre's *Être Suprême*"—if only Robespierre had appeared, he reflected, with an old Bible under his arm, and told his countrymen to become Protestants, he might have succeeded.

12. The Clergy under the Terror

What happened to the clergy under the Terror and the de-Christianization? The Convention did not condemn the practice of religion: it proscribed priests. Its multifarious penal legislation can be summed up in two grim formulae: deportation (and after October, death) for refusing the oath of Liberty, and deportation for any priest on the mere demand of six citizens. This meant in practice that the constitutional clergy were as vulnerable as the orthodox—and they had not had time to flee or go underground.

Thirty to forty thousand non-jurors emigrated, principally to England, Spain, and the Papal dominions. Since nine-tenths of the émigrés were seculars, it has been suggested that the regulars found it easier to come to terms with the Revolution. This was so, obviously, with those who were grateful for their release from monastic obligations. As for the others, we must remember that they had not come under such direct public notice as the parochial clergy. The oath to the Civil Constitution had not been required of them and, by returning to their original homes, many had escaped from the environment where they had been known as monks in recent years. Regulars, in general, had less reason to flee from France than seculars.

We have a great deal of evidence about the sufferings of the clergy who remained in France, but as yet no precise statistics. Perhaps two thousand were executed, perhaps as many as five thousand, while many more were imprisoned. Persecution was intense in certain areas and left others untouched. In nine departments there were no capital sentences on priests, in two only one, in many only two. The worst savageries were in zones of civil war: 135 priests and monks were massacred at Lyon in November 1793; eighty-three were shot in one day

106

at the Champ des Martyrs near Angers. The bitter details of Carrier's mass drownings at Nantes are well known; so too are the orderly processes of the justice of the Terror at Paris— the dirty straw and the smell of urine at the Conciergerie or the Égalité, the daily list for trial, Fouquier-Tinville's rhetoric, the cart rumbling to the scaffold. But the hulks of Rochefort were grimmer and claimed more clergy as victims than both Carrier and the Revolutionary Tribunal—of the 850 priests (from the North and East and Belgium) imprisoned in the three old slaving ships, only 274 survived.

Nuns were not spared. Sixteen Carmelites of Compiègne were sent up to Paris to be despatched; there were the Filles de la Charité of Arras, the Ursulines of Valenciennes, the thirty-two nuns executed by the Commission d'Orange, and numerous individual victims. What danger could these simple women have been to the Republic? Of the seven Parisian nuns guillotined from May to July 1794, three had refused to reveal the identity of the refractory priest who had been saying their masses, one had been concealing the papers of a re-fractory, one had corresponded with her émigré brother, another had been found in possession of royalist tracts, and the abbess of Montmartpe, seventy-two years of age, was accused of making "exactions" upon her "vassals". No doubt injustices are inevitable when a nation is fighting for survival, but (royalist tracts apart) how can one justify these executions? And how can one explain those of the *abbé* Broquet, chaplain of Notre-Dame, eighty years of age, of Gravier, constitutional *vicaire* of Saint-Roch, who had been wounded in the march on the Tuileries as a corporal in the National Guard, of the scholarly old Jansenist Dom Deforis, who naively told the Tribunal that he never took oaths on principle, and who was described by Fouquier-Tinville as "one of those criminals who, armed with a cross, torches, and daggers, have spilt human blood from one end of Europe to another . . ."? There were, too, the lay folk who were put to death for concealing non-jurors, like Modeste Babin of Poitiers, betrayed by two cowardly priests, brothers, whom she had assisted. She knew

Pierre Verdier, the executioner, well, as they had occupied ad-
joining seats in the church of Saint-Michel in the old days;
when he died sixty years later he was holding the cross she
gave him on the steps of the guillotine. This is what the
Revolution was like. In our zeal for statistics and geographical
and social analysis we must beware of making trivial the overwhelming business of dying.

The highlight of a de-Christianization ceremony was the
spectacle of a priest abjuring his vocation. Since, whatever
oaths of loyalty they undertook, the clergy remained subject
to deportation at the whim of any half a dozen individuals, and
to death for the slightest suspicion of anti-revolutionary
activities, the de-Christianizers had weapons to hand to break
the will of their victims. When the Convention allowed the
Department and Commune of Paris to bring in Gobel, the
constitutional bishop, and eleven of his episcopal council, to
renounce the functions of their ministry (17 brumaire II, 7
November 1793), and encouraged Thomas Lindet, Bishop of
the Eure, and other ecclesiastical representatives to follow
suit, it was giving a sort of official approval to the use of
such clerical abdications as tests of *civisme*. Six days later a
formal decree authorized local authorities to receive and
record them. Large numbers of clergy, whether publicly or by
private declaration, allowed themselves to be de-Christianized
in this fashion. Inevitably, most were constitutionals, for they
were available to be victimized, having had no occasion to
emigrate and no opportunity to go into hiding. In spite of
the importunity of his colleagues in the Convention, Grégoire
stood firm, but in his diocese only thirty-two out of his 300
priests were unshaken. Of the eighty-five constitutional
bishops, forty-seven abdicated; so too did 267 out of the four
or five hundred clergy of Paris, and a majority of the constitutional priests of the Pas de Calais, the Loir-et-Cher and
the Oise. A realistic estimate for the total of abdications in the
whole of France is 20,000. Whatever else the de-Christianizers
had failed to do, at least they succeeded in wrecking and dis-
crediting the Constitutional Church.

Recent work on the statistics of clerical "abdications" supports the broad conclusion, already fairly obvious, that few could have been spontaneous: the vast majority were made under pressure, in desperate and feverish circumstances. Of the 629 known cases in Provence, 579 can be dated, and of these no less than 494 fall in the months of ventôse and germinal, coinciding with the wave of anti-clerical manifestations stirred up by the *représentants en mission*. In Paris the great drive is concentrated in brumaire, frimaire, and the first half of nivôse, reaching a paroxysm at the time of the Festival of Reason. And it was in sizeable towns that the de-Christianizers could most efficiently organize their pressure; the statistics confirm its effectiveness (for example, 142 abdications in Marseille alone, almost a clean sweep of clergy available to be persecuted). The geographical incidence of *les prêtres abdicataires* sometimes coincides with the map of traditional religion and irreligion in France: in the Basses-Alpes, of six districts the three mountain areas alone are practically unscathed, and in the Alpes-Maritimes there were only two cases, as against something like 300 in the Bouches-du-Rhône. But when a complete survey is finally compiled it will necessarily be an indication of the places where the confrontation was strongest, not of Catholic and Jacobin France, though a comparison of the two maps may tell us something of the support that the faithful laity could give to clerical morale in the days of oppression. Incomplete though they are, the statistics provide us with the occasional sharp, illuminating contrast; they reflect, for example, the lax discipline of the Capuchins and of the canons-regular of Sainte-Geneviève under the *ancien régime* as compared with the austerity of the Sulpiciens and the priests of the Missions Étrangères. But the most interesting of all the correlations is both illuminating and puzzling. What are we to think of the fact that few younger priests seem to have abdicated, as compared with large numbers in the 40–60 age group? Was it that theological training was improving under the *ancien régime,* or is it simply that young men are more resilient?—is there some subtle connexion, conditioned by age, with the politically effective groups in the population, or did the younger clergy simply find it easier to hide or take to flight?

It is hard to be confident about general explanations, for there were different kinds of abdication, and it is important to distinguish. Of the forty-seven constitutional bishops who formally gave up their episcopal status, only twenty-three actually apostasized. Gobel before the Convention chose his words carefully; he said he was renouncing the functions of his ministry, since there "ought not to be any longer any other *public* cult but that of liberty and sacred equality", and the documents he handed over were those of his election and enthronization as bishop. It was Chaumette who added the gloss that he was giving up his priesthood and, by remaining silent, Gobel condemned himself. This distinction, between abandoning one's vocation and proposing in deference to the "general will" to renounce its public exercise, is important. In some places the clergy agreed among themselves to write privately to the authorities declaring their intention to cease performing liturgical functions hoping thereby to escape further humiliations. In others priests handed over their letters of ordination while pronouncing a common formula, evidence of the compulsion they were under and of their joint responsibility; some individuals resigned but declared that they had "lost" their letters of priesthood, or they evaded signing the register. One *curé* handed over only the papers concerning his appointment to the parish, but covered up this subterfuge by the fine de-Christianizing gesture of handing in a chalice as an extra; another insisted on signing the register for the abandonment of feudal titles instead of that of clerical abdications. *Curé* Coffin of Arras wrote to the Department to say that he had stayed at his post in the parish so long as his country needed him, braving the "rage of the aristocracy", but that "now the people want no more religious observances— very well then, I retire; my presence at Arras would be more dangerous than useful". And he told them where to find the vicarage key. He was not unfrocking himself. He was simply departing from a place where he was not wanted.

Some local de-Christianizers would be content with nothing less than the handing over of letters of priesthood. Even so, to yield to this demand was not always downright cowardice or apostasy. These letters were signed by prelates of the *ancien régime,* "the unworthy signatures of . . . beings who have become the shame of the human species". Doctors too were sometimes required to hand over their certificates, because they had the royal arms and the name of the "tyrant" upon them. In the Department of the Vienne, most of the priests who surrendered their letters went on quietly with their ministry, and there are examples of the kind elsewhere. They had convinced themselves that the handing over of their ecclesiastical certificates was a gesture of repudiation of "aristocracy" and the *ancien régime,* rather than an abdication of their own sacred functions.

There were those, of course, who specifically recorded their intention of repudiating their vocation; they handed in their "letters of imposture", they confessed to having been "charlatans", and turned their backs on the "vampires" with whom they had consorted; they declared that they had been ordained merely to please their families, or to promote the cause of "philosophy" or natural religion. A *curé* of Bourges, more inventive than most, expressed his relief that his tongue would "no more be soiled by the Gothic chants of the former Church, which resemble rather the songs of nocturnal birds than hymns in honour of the Supreme Being". One suspects, sometimes, that this fruity anti-clerical invective was dictated by the de-Christianizers, or has been embellished for the record. However this may have been, there is no doubt that most abdications were insincere. "Most ecclesiastics unfrocked themselves", writes M. Dommanget, the historian of de-Christianization at Beauvais, "as a tactical manœuvre, through fear, driven by necessity".

As a final proof that he had abandoned his vocation, a priest might marry. The de-Christianizers (except some unreasonable ones at Auch) seemed to have accepted this evidence as conclusive. A former ecclesiastic of Sens wrote to the terrorist Albitte urging him to slacken his measures of surveillance against priests, so that they could have opportunities to look around for marriage partners. "You know how vital it is to the Republic to get priests not subject to deportation to marry. It is, perhaps, the only way of effacing their claim to a special status in the eyes of the vulgar." This was the view of the Convention. By a decree of 25 brumaire (15 November 1793), once a priest's banns were called he was no longer subject to deportation or imprisonment.

Some of the clergy, orthodox and constitutional, married to save their lives. To salve their consciences, they might make it evident by their choice that sexual promptings had not driven them to matrimony or, better still, they might manage to find a partner who would agree to allow the marriage to remain unconsummated. What started as a fictitious union might, amid the fears and loneliness of the days of Terror, become real. This is how Père Grandjean, former Provincial of the Dominicans of Paris, a Jansenist who had campaigned against the Civil Constitution of the Clergy, became married to a nun of his order, and the father of two children.

Marriage being what it is and the times being troubled, motives were inevitably mixed. By taking a wife, a priest might do more than just save himself from jail—simultaneously he might be qualifying for a post in the cantonal administration or as a librarian or teacher. At the beginning of October 1793, the club at Compiègne wanted a rule that unmarried priests would be denied all official employment, unless they could prove that the object of their affections, "too bogged down in old and absurd prejudices", had rejected their proposal. The idea of the married cleric as an ambiguous, discredited figure is often very far from the truth. In republican areas, by marrying, a priest won friends, relatives, and acceptance in society. And even when fear of death or of poverty were the manifest driving forces towards matrimony, this did not rule out genuine inclination, so that anti-clericals had further matter for declamation when the bride was younger or prettier than they thought was appropriate.

Indeed, the insistence of the de-Christianizers must sometimes have been the excuse for marriage, rather than the real reason. To some clergy, the possibility of taking a wife had not been unforeseen before the Terror made it something like a necessity. A host of pamphlets and an occasional *cahier* in 1789 had asked for the abolition of the rule of clerical celibacy. Marriage was described as a natural right, which a man was not allowed to forego, however willingly. With Rousseauistic *sensibilité* it was argued that true happiness can only be found in the bosom of a virtuous family. The education of youth, it was said, and the spiritual guidance of women, ought to be in the hands of family men who had a stake in the country and ties of mutual obligation with their fellows. *Rendons les prêtres citoyens* was the title of one of the pamphlets.

In this propaganda Augustinian doctrines of the sinfulness of carnal desire were confuted. Some day a thesis will be written about the French Revolution's naive enthusiasm for sex—about Sylvain Maréchal's Temple of Hymen, where young lovers kiss the transparent urn containing the ashes of the two most virtuous spouses of the canton, where the only vows are vows against abstinence, and the only penance is to "make love again, better"; about Fouché's Temple of Love at Nevers, where husbands and wives swore eternal fidelity, like Baucis and Philemon; about the hymns and poems, often by married clerics, rejoicing in the victory of "chaste amours" over "selfish celibacy", on to the *Fête des Époux* under the Directory, "where duties ennoble and purify the pleasures, and the pleasures temper the austerity of the most holy duties"— invented by François de Neufchâteau, a libertine if ever there was one. There was a spirit of sexual release in the Revolution, and it was this rather than crude anti-clericalism which gave special point to the enthusiasm with which everybody observed that St Peter had been a married man and, indeed, probably all the other Apostles as well, except St John.

So far as ecclesiastical law went, the obstacles, though

explicit, were not regarded as irremovable. The rule of priestly celibacy, as distinct from the vow of chastity of the monks, was defined as "a simple condition laid down by the Church for the exercise of sacerdotal duties . . . which [the Church] can dispense with when she wishes". (These terms can hardly be suspect, as they come from the rigorist Presbytery of the Constitutional Church at Paris, anxious to condemn the marriages so many priests had contracted.) It was also argued that legally clerical marriage was possible already. *Curé* Rémi Vinchon, of the District of Bar-sur-Aube, who in May 1790 declared himself married by private contract to Marie-Anne Puisset, justified his action by saying that he was not breaking a law of the State, but only a rule of the Council of Trent, which had never been accepted by the government in France. He was exercising, he claimed, one of the "natural impre-scriptable rights of man". (There was evidence, four months later, that he had exercised these rights five months before the wedding.) Therefore, he said, he was marrying by contract while awaiting more precise regulations from the National Assembly. In the autumn of 1791 the National Assembly did, in fact, commit itself indirectly to a ruling. In September, it promised to maintain the payment of pensions to monks and nuns who married; in October, by passing to "the order of the day", it gave virtual approval to a proposal to extend this principle to all ecclesiastical benefice holders. Already, the *abbé* de Cournaud, a professor of the Collège de France, had gone to the municipality with his *de facto* wife to legitimize their two sons through a contract of civil marriage. A few more clerical marriages—true marriages, with the nuptial blessing—followed. At the church of Sainte-Marguerite in Paris, Aubert the *vicaire* had his marriage blessed by Bernard the sacristan, who in turn contracted marriage with the blessing of Aubert. In November 1792 Lindet, Bishop of the Eure, had his banns called. By now the war and the Emigration were being used by patriots as a proof of their arguments against celibacy, for it was a "rootless" pastorate that had deserted to join the enemies of France.

In the atmosphere in which the de-Christianization was to flourish, but before the actual campaign began, the movement for clerical marriage gained impetus. On 18 August 1793, Bishop Torné of Bourges celebrated the marriage of Fargin, one of his metropolitan vicars and commander of the National Guard, giving a discourse in which he regretted that his age prevented him from co-operating in so salutary a reform (later on, he demonstrated that the obstacle was not insuperable). On 10 September, Torné presided over the wedding of two of his *curés*. On 22 September, Pontard, Bishop of the Dordogne, presented his wife to the Convention—"poor in fortune, rich in virtue, from the class of the *sans-culottes*, wherein is found candour and amiable simplicity". On 24 September at Poitiers, de Pigonneau, an ex-noble and canon, married a charming young girl at the cathedral, in the presence of all the local officials. Allowing time for preliminary arrangements, these marriages seem too early to have been the direct result of the pressure of the de-Christianizers. The historian of religious affairs in the Vienne emphasizes the sincerity of many of the priests of the department who married; they did not wish to abandon their ecclesiastical vocation, and when forced to abdicate, they did so unwillingly. They were wanting, "not a de-Christianization, but a Reformation".

How many priests married? We can only guess. Grégoire, who would wish to limit the dimensions of what he regarded as a scandal, estimated that there were two thousand. The actual requests for absolution made to the Legation in Napoleon's time came to a total of 3,224 (of which 2,313 had been seculars and 911 monks); there were also requests from 272 nuns. The findings of local historians (Sévèstre counted 500 in Normandy, Pisani 200 at Paris, Dommanget 50 in the Oise, while the count runs at just over 100 each for the towns of Lyon, Bourges, Versailles, and Amiens) suggest that there must have been many more whose names did not reach the records of the Legation. What we can be sure, however, is that not all were cowards or weaklings; indeed, the mere listing of the professions under the Empire of the three thousand applicants for absolution leaves an impression of men of character and abilities. There are five prefects, twelve sub-prefects, one general, one financial expert who later became Minister of Finance, there is the archivist of the *Conseil d'État,* and Fouché's chief assistant at the police; there are many mayors of communes, professors at *collèges* and *lycées.* Nor must we assume that all were deliberately unfaithful to their vocation as they saw it. External pressures and lures are only part of the story; there were emotions and aspirations working within, imposing themselves upon men who, ever since that fatal January of 1791, had been trapped in a chaos of civil strife and hatred that bewildered their understanding.

The de-Christianization did not penetrate everywhere. In some parishes in the Haute-Loire and the Jura the orthodox clergy ruled their flocks as they had in the days before the Civil Constitution was heard of. The municipal assembly of Pont-l'Evêque in Normandy put up a great show of enthusiasm for the revolutionary cults (run by the ex-constitutional *curé),* to camouflage the fact that the parish was carrying on under its refractory priest all the time. In some towns the nuns of the hospitals stayed at their posts through the Terror. The decree of 18 August 1792 had ordered them to do so, though their religious costume was suppressed, and in October 1793, the oath of Liberty-Equality was imposed on them. In Paris the Sisters of Saint-Thomas-de-Villeneuve kept their orphanages going until the Convention nationalized them in July 1795, and the Augustines stayed at the Hôtel-Dieu, though they had to wear tricolour sashes and attend dances to allay the suspicions of patriots. Even in towns where the de-Christianizers ran rampant, there were priests in disguise exercising a clandestine ministry, like the "chaplains of the guillotine" in Paris, penetrating into the prisons or giving absolution as the tumbrils went by. Though local histories are full of stories about their adventures, our information about the priests who exercised a clandestine ministry is, in the nature of the case, fragmentary. But there can be no mystery about their motives. The Revolution, which imposed upon so many clergy choices of impossible, unjust complexity, to these men had at last brought a plain decision between clear alternatives. They had an opportunity to demonstrate their loyalty to their vocation and to the person upon whose life and suffering the Christian hope is founded. The *abbé* Coudrin of Poitiers, disguised as a workman, when challenged by a sentry to give the name of his master, replied "Rabbi".

"Rabbi? I don't know him."
"C'est dommage, vous y gagneriez."

13. *Thermidor to Brumaire*

The men of 1789 had regarded Church and State as insep-
arable. To them the assembled nation represented, in some
sense, the *ecclesia*, and it had seemed natural to "nationalize
Catholicism and put it at the service of the new order". Two
years later, their assumptions crumbled away when half the
clergy of France rejected the Civil Constitution. At this very
time, across the Atlantic, the First Congress was passing the
first amendment to the Constitution: "Congress shall make
no law respecting an establishment of religion, or prohibiting
the free exercise thereof". In the end, the separation of
Church and State, a clean incisive formula in the clear air
of the new world on the edge of the American wilderness,
was to be accepted in France as a smeary inevitability, the
outcome of miscalculations and frenzies. We have seen how
the Revolution abandoned and persecuted the Constitutional
Church which it had founded. The Terror ended with the fall
of Robespierre in Thermidor (July 1794). Slowly the prisons
were opened and the habit of invoking the penal laws against
the clergy faded. Further persecution of Catholicism would be
futile, perhaps dangerous. On the other hand, after the Terror
and the de-Christianization, the continued existence of a
State Church in revolutionary France was an absurdity. In
September 1794 the Convention officially ended clerical
salaries, which were not being paid anyway. On 3 ventôse
year III (21 February 1795), the decree of Boissy d'Anglas
was passed: bells and other external signs of religion, including
ecclesiastical dress, were prohibited; the Republic was not to
recognize nor pay for any religion but, according to article
VII of the Declaration of Rights, it guaranteed the free
exercise of all.

This decree, which formally recognized the fact of the separation of Church and State, seemed more important to contemporaries as a simple police regulation allowing Catholics to assemble unobtrusively for worship. In December Grégoire had complained that revolutionary liberty seemed to add up to nothing more than the freedom to practise religion in one's own home—"The Declaration of Rights, the Constitution, the laws published so majestically, have as their sole aim the statutory establishment of the fact that, in my own room, I can do as I please". But when the decree of 21 February became known, there was a rush by a courageous minority to open the churches again, in so far as churches remained available, for some had been sold, some demolished, and others were in a dangerous state of ill-repair. "Queues at mass and queues at the doors of bakers' shops", said the *Courier de l'égalité* grimly, linking together these twin phenomena of republican decadence. On Easter Day the shops of Paris were closed and some of the churches were open. At Sedan on 26 March a procession of women, brooms on shoulder and a drummer in the lead, went to the cathedral to clean out the rubbish left by various revolutionary festivals, including the débris of the Statue of Liberty, which someone had knocked down ten days before. At Clermont, *curé* Glaize, who was earning his living as a sheep trader, recorded in his diary that he started saying masses again in April. It took courage to come out into the open so soon after the tempest. At Lille, in August, the *abbé* Cuitte tried to say mass and was rescued from the ensuing riot by the mayor, the National Guard, and troops of the line. The writ of article VII of the Declaration of Rights did not run everywhere.

Along with the liberty of religious exercise the laws also prescribed the liberty of educational choice, another theoretical freedom which now became a reality—albeit precariously—for churchmen. Parents who disliked the official institutions, from which religion was excluded, were able to send their children to be educated privately, and many clergy were able to maintain themselves by opening schools or finding employment as private tutors. "It is under the Directory", writes M. Latreille, "that the educational dispute between religious and lay influences begins—this interminable dispute which was to be one of the most intractable problems and one of the most characteristic features of the spiritual life of modern France, right up to our own day".

But such freedom as the Church enjoyed was grudgingly conceded. Sunday had to be a working day, with the *décadi* as the holiday. Local authorities exercised surveillance over religious services; preachers found that some of the most assiduous attenders at their sermons were police spies. Priests were subject to tests of civic submission and were held responsible, under threat of arbitrary deportation, for any infringements of the rules against bells and "exterior signs". Those who kept schools were watched by a local "*jury d'instruction*", and were in trouble if they took lessons on the *décadi* or gave holidays on Sunday.

And official toleration, limited as it was, did not last. The elections of the summer of 1797 were won by royalists and moderate republicans. In the countryside priests who had remained in hiding distrustfully suddenly emerged. The bells were rung again. Three of the five Directors, La Revellière, Barras, and Reubell, called in the army to break the menace of a political reaction allied with a religious revival. By the coup of Fructidor (14 September 1797), they purged the assemblies and kept power in the hands of the republican old guard. The days of religious persecution returned. Priests who wished to conduct services were required to swear a sinister oath of "hatred of royalty", and the Directory took to itself the power to deport ecclesiastics by simple administrative order. This procedure, arbitrary in itself, was applied in the newly-annexed Belgian departments in the astonishingly unjust form of collective deportation lists; they proved unworkable and, of the eight thousand priests listed, less than a thousand were actually arrested. Thirty Belgian priests and over two hundred from France were brutally transported to Cayenne,

where most died of fever. Two thousand others were imprisoned at Rochefort and on the islands of Ré and Oléron.
There were few executions. The Directors wished to strike
terror without creating martyrs. Theirs was a cold-blooded
persecution, unsupported by the outrages and Rabelaisian
guffaws of a popular de-Christianization. Its chief effect was
to ensure the irreconcilable distrust and hatred of Catholics
for the régime; the way was being made easier for Bonaparte.

During the two and a half years of quasi-toleration which
followed the decree of Boissy d'Anglas, the Constitutional
Church struggled to regain coherent existence. At the beginning of 1795 it seemed that the de-Christianizers had
overthrown it. Of the eighty-two bishops of 1792, ten were
dead (six on the scaffold), twenty-three had apostasized, and
another twenty-four had renounced their letters of priesthood.
A majority of the lower clergy, perhaps as many as five in
every six, had in one way or another given up their vocation.
In royalist and Catholic areas the faithful minority faced the
threats and daggers of *chouans* and "brigands"; in republican
departments they were pursued by the malice and derision
of the practitioners of de-Christianization. The constitutionals were committed beyond recall to the cause of the
Revolution. As a symbol of their complicity men pointed to
the fact that, of the forty-one ecclesiastics in the Convention,
no less than twenty-two had voted for the death of the King—
if one cared to insist on the calculation, they had provided the
regicides with their majority. Yet the cause for which they
had sacrificed so much had disowned them. More than this,
the Revolution itself had changed: it was no longer the dawn
of regeneration it had appeared to be half a dozen years ago.
Its supporters were now a vested material interest, a league
of officials, senior military men and buyers of Church property.
The wars of liberty with their conscription and inflation continued, seemingly endlessly, while the ideal itself was being
forgotten. Priests who had taken the oath to the Civil Constitution of the Clergy out of revolutionary idealism or patriotic

duty, and those who had taken it to obtain security or prestige, were equally disillusioned.

Yet, once religious services could be publicly held again, a revival came, here and there, in widely scattered places, and essentially at the parochial level, wherever there was a group of faithful laity brave enough to take advantage of the law and a priest with the courage to come forward to celebrate. The researches of Pisani show how the revival began at Paris. In the parishes of Saint-Laurent, Saint-Philippe du Roule, Saint-Eustache, Saint-Germain l'Auxerrois, and Notre-Dame lay associations can be seen at work, approaching the authorities for the use of a church building and inviting a priest to take office as *curé*. At Notre Dame the association decided to pay a parish priest, a sacristan, two *suisses,* four choirmen and one player of the *serpent,* with the proviso that they would not accept any priest who had married, or any choristers "who had prostituted their voices by singing in theatres". The clergy who emerged to exercise the parochial ministry were men of character. There was Fernbach, the ex-Dominican, who blandly informed the authorities that he had removed the inscription to the *"Être Suprême"* from his church because the law forbade "exterior signs of religion"; Margarita and Bougière, who had defied the de-Christianizers; *curé* Poupart of Saint-Eustache, who had kept his parish clergy together throughout the persecutions; Corpet of Saint-Germain l'Auxerrois, who thought himself unworthy because he had given up his letters of priesthood, but was too much loved by his parishioners to be allowed to remain in the wilderness; there was Baillet, of a prosperous merchant family, who had chivalrously come forward to be ordained in the days of the Terror.

The strength and persistence of the revival varied. In some towns lay support was limited to respectable citizens, in others, there was some popular enthusiasm. If an official report is to be believed, in the small manufacturing town of Elbeuf three quarters of the citizens, including practically all the "lower classes", were agitating for the restoration of the

Constitutional Church. A great deal would depend upon the quality of the clerical leadership available. Bayeaux was fortunate in having the charismatic Michael Moulland, who drew crowds to the cathedral. Paris was fortunate too at the start, but some of the most effective *curés* soon decided to turn to the orthodox churchmen to ask for reintegration, and the Parisian revival declined. There were broad areas of France where the Constitutional Church had no contacts—in the West and other clerical areas, where it had never succeeded in putting down roots, and in the departments of the centre (the Oise, the Yonne, the Cher and the Allier), because it never recovered from the onslaughts of the de-Christianizers. The Civil Constitution of the Clergy had provided no machinery for central control or decision making in the Church, and the two dozen faithful bishops who remained had been for long in prison or in hiding, out of touch with their clergy. Apart from the leadership of one heroic individual, what had once been a Church would have revived as a few isolated dioceses and a scattering of unconnected parishes outside them.

This leadership came from Henri Grégoire, constitutional Bishop of Blois, one of the few men who lived through the Revolution without betraying a friend or abandoning a principle. Humourless and obstinate, but transfigured by his intense convictions, he steered an undeviating course while the whole world around him was tacking through shoal and storm. He had been absent when the death of the King was voted, but made himself a regicide by publishing his opinion —"the end of a wild beast, the cessation of a plague, the death of a King, are motives of joy for humanity". Throughout the Terror he was at his place on the benches of the Convention, defying the priest-haters. "Religion is outside your province", he told his fellow-deputies, "I have been elected by the people to be a bishop, but neither from them nor from you is my mission derived". He never retracted his oath to the Civil Constitution of the Clergy, and when Bonaparte and then the Bourbons came to rule he remained a republican.

Once the decree of Boissy d'Anglas was passed Grégoire

took the lead in forming a standing council of bishops at Paris (the *évêques réunis*). There were Royer, Savine, and himself, all deputies to the Convention, and Desbois and Gratien, newly released from prison. On 15 March 1795 they issued a profession of faith, and on 1 May they said mass at the church of Saint-Médard and declared the parish open again. Bishop Desbois had a private fortune which was used to found a newspaper, the *Annales de la Religion*. Grégoire himself issued a pastoral letter, in which he boldly denounced the de-Christianizers, vicious persecutors egged on by the applause of "shameless and crapulous women". In an encyclical dated 13 December 1795 the bishops laid down a new system of Church organization. Twelve *curés* of each episcopal town and its surrounding countryside were to assemble to set up a Presbytery; where there was no bishop to co-operate with them, the Presbytery would organize a new election—*curés* would put up the names of candidates, the balloting to be by parishes, and within each parish all the faithful over the age of twenty-one would be entitled to vote. This new church polity (with its subsequent modifications) had its defects: more especially, the authority of bishops was not easily made compatible with that of presbyteries. In 1796, the Presbytery of Paris prevented Bishop Royer from taking over Notre-Dame ("despotism begins when the will of one becomes the law for all"), and in 1798 it set up its own newspaper, the *Journal religieux*, and changed the election procedure for the diocese. But as an expedient the new system worked. Thirty bishops and representatives of numerous presbyteries attended a National Council in 1797, and three years later there were fifty-eight constitutional bishops, leaving only twenty-nine sees vacant. By then, however, Bonaparte had decided on the Concordat with Rome and the days of the Constitutional Church were numbered.

Though Grégoire gave his Church a profession of faith and a system of government he could not provide it with a philosophical ethos, a practical and theological justification for separate existence. In its origin it had been a national

institution, keeper of the conscience of the French people and
its collaborator in a patriotic regeneration; now the connection
with the nation was ended and the regeneration had proved
an illusion. In the days of the Civil Constitution men had
yearned for an ecclesiastical order purged from the abuses
that accompanied excessive riches and freed from dependence
on Rome: now Rome was in eclipse and the riches had been
confiscated. So the Constitutional Church stood revealed as an
historical accident, neither the Church of a nation nor the
Church of a reformation. In 1796, Panisset, one of the bishops,
made his peace with the refractories; so too did four of the
newly-established *curés* of Paris and two of Grégoire's own
episcopal vicars. These were important defections. Had the
orthodox bishops been generous in their reception of repentant
constitutionals, there would have been more.

The story of the refractory clergy in exile is a sad one, but
the saddest thing about it is the way in which misfortune had
corroded the last vestiges of charity in the minds of some of
the prelates who had fled from France. Thémines, Bishop of
Blois, Cheylus of Bayeux, La Tour du Pin Montauban of
Auch, and Marbeuf of Lyon proved as insensitive in assessing
the motives of jurors to the Civil Constitution as the Constituent Assembly had been in devising the oath originally.
They imposed public retractions of a most humiliating kind
("buried in the deep abyss of every crime . . . for long dead
to Grace", was Thémines' formula), penances, and embarass-
ing delays before reintegration. Theirs was the severity of
exiles—or, to put it bluntly, of men who had chosen safety.
Marbeuf, a prelate of the court in pre-Revolution days, was
far away at Lubeck when he imposed a sentence of three
months suspension upon an heroic *curé* who, in January 1794
retracted all his oaths and informed municipality, District,
Department, and Convention that he had done so. By contrast,
Emery, Superior of Saint-Sulpice, and Moreau, Bishop of
Mâcon, asked no retractions—they refused even to use the
word. Both of them had stayed in France and had known fear
and despair themselves in the prisons of the Terror.

The orthodox as well as the constitutionals had reason to regret Marbeuf's intransigence and to welcome the moderation of Emery. In the "thaw" that followed the decree of Boissy d'Anglas there was a rush for church buildings, and on 30 May 1795 the government imposed a declaration of "submission to the laws of the Republic" on the priests who proposed to make use of them. The old disputes that had raged over the oath of Liberty-Equality of August 1792 now revived. Marbeuf was against the submission, though his vicar-general in the diocese of Lyon allowed it under "the express reserve" of matters concerning faith and morals and provided there was no sharing of church buildings with constitutionals. Emery regretted that the legislators had failed to consult experts in casuistry; but he authorized the declaration, pointing out that "submission" did not imply approbation, that the laws included freedom of religious exercise, and that the Church could refuse its sacraments to citizens who made use of the legislation concerning divorce. But in September the government made an even wilder demonstration of its ignorance of technical casuistry by changing to the formula, "I recognize the universality of French citizens as sovereign, and I promise submission and obedience to the laws of the Republic". This affirmation was forbidden at Lyon and condemned by the Faculty of Theology at Louvain. Even Emery was hesitant. If it meant that, in fact, sovereignty in France rested in the people, he would subscribe; if it meant that sovereignty ought to be in the people, he could not do so, though he was pleased to acknowledge that those who preferred the teachings of Suarez and Gerson to the principles of Bossuet would do otherwise. On the other hand, Clermont-Tonnerre, exiled Bishop of Châlons-sur-Marne, wrote to his clergy in France *ordering* them to submit. He was not one of those exiles who pushed others into the firing line. He was prepared to pay for his immunity by accepting extra burdens on his conscience.

After the coup of Fructidor the most lurid of the revolutionary oaths was imposed on the clergy, that of "hatred of royalty and anarchy". Though royalists were loud in their denunciations, this fantastic formula did not prove quite so difficult as more precise affirmations concerning the positive acceptance of laws might have been. Emery said that he would not take the oath himself, but was glad others could do so. Clermont-Tonnerre again ordered his clergy to conform, and permission to do so was given by the Archbishop of Paris and some other *émigré* prelates. If "hate" is taken in an unemotional, purely intellectual sense, if "royalty" is limited to the sort of régime that the Bourbon exiles proposed to restore, and if the bloodshed that would ensue from any major attempt on their part was made the primary object of abhorrence, the oath became something like an expression of submission to the Republic as it existed. This had been the point of Emery's remark about the advisability of calling in a professional casuist. Professional advice would have warned the successive revolutionary governments that oaths should be limited to guaranteeing obedience to a *de facto* régime. As in other things, Bonaparte learnt from the Revolution's mistakes. After his *coup d'état,* the declaration required by the law of 7 nivôse (27 December 1799) was simply (though still not casuistically perfect), "I promise fidelity to the Constitution".

The reckless phraseology of the revolutionary oaths is surprising. As La Harpe sardonically observed in his treatise on revolutionary "fanaticism" in 1797, it was hard to think of anything further to abjure except, perhaps, one might swear "hatred of the plague". Such incompetent draughtsmanship, indeed, makes one wonder if the primary objective really was to ensure compliance. The successive legislators of revolutionary France, in whatever corruption or cruelty they were confounded, were still haunted by the revolutionary ideal of universality. They shied away from the possibility that honest men could disagree with them. When they devised oaths they told themselves that they were asking only for submission, but subconsciously they were asking also for allegiance; and a refusal was more than a difference of opinion, it was a betrayal.

In Joubert's words, it was a case of *"Sois mon ami ou je te tue"*. In this sense royalists had justification for their argument that the oaths could only be taken by revolutionary enthusiasts. Not that they cared about the content of the oaths: they were simply using every means to ensure that Catholics hated the régime, playing out the cards in the Church's hand now that they had none left in their own. "You would tremble", wrote Emery in a letter of November 1796, "if you could see how disastrous to religion is the unreasonableness of certain people who are dominated by foolish preoccupations of counter-revolution, and for whom religion, instead of being an end, is just a means".

As between the subconscious dishonesty of revolutionaries and the conscious dishonesty of royalists, the orthodox clergy were under intolerable pressures. Those who wanted the Church to survive preached to them on the text *in dubietate libertas*: those who wished to see the Government overthrown replied with elaborations upon the tag, *in dubio iurare non licet*. But through these bitter confusions one conclusion was becoming evident—the Church must dissociate itself from any particular political system. "The Catholic religion", wrote the Bishop of Boulogne in October 1797, "can coexist with all forms of legitimate government". The *abbé* Coste, in a *Manuel pour Missionnaires,* declared that "the Christian religion has always submitted to the different forms that revolutions have given to temporal governments, and its ministers have never had any right to take part in those revolutions. They obeyed the authorities which arose, whether they were established by God in his mercy, or permitted by him in his wrath". Boisgelin, the *émigré* Archbishop of Aix, said that the oath to accept republican government was impossible to him as a nobleman, but as a priest, he "would take it tomorrow. Everything comes to one point—must religion perish because the government has changed?" The mistake of the Directory was to ignore these sentiments and to prefer anticlerical growling and bristling to the genuine neutrality in religious affairs which might have brought about a pacification. In the summer of

1796 the Papacy itself was ready to issue clear instructions to the faithful to render obedience to the *de facto* rulers of France. A letter, *Pastoralis sollicitudo,* was prepared, and had the Directory been more supple in diplomacy and less blinded by anticlericalism, the document would have been published formally. The opportunity passed. General Bonaparte, triumphant in Italy, brooded on the lesson and on the folly of his masters.

The revival of the Constitutional Church had been characterized by the spontaneous refounding of parishes locally and by Grégoire's determined leadership from the centre. By contrast, orthodox Catholicism lacked leadership and was less successful at the level of the parochial group. When orthodox clergy exercised the legal right to officiate in a church, they ran greater risks than the constitutionals, for they were the especial target for sly persecution by the secular authorities during the period of official toleration, and for open persecution after the coup of Fructidor. In some places the centre for worship was found in communities of nuns which had quietly re-established themselves—as in Paris, under Mme de Soyecourt in the ruined convent of the Carmelites, with its unhappy, sacred memories of the September Massacres, and under Marie-Félicité Melon in the old convent of the Rue Saint-Denis, where a group of nuns and their boarding-school provided a refuge for refractory priests.

In a dozen dioceses or more the chief instrument of spiritual revival was the "mission", which was independently invented in the dioceses of Lyon and Tournai in 1794. The *abbé* Linsolas, vicar-general of Marbeuf, who introduced the system at Lyon, was consciously imitating the organization used by French missionaries in the Far East. Priests wearing lay dress, not only to conform to the law but also to disguise their activities, were escorted from village to village by "catechists", and in each place a *chef de paroisse* divided the faithful into groups to hear masses in private houses, "reserving the least prudent to the last night". The heroic adventures of this religious "underground" were mingled—as is the way of human nature under stress—with petty scandal; peasants refused to pay their dues once they had performed their Easter duties, *chefs de paroisse* tried to "act the *curé*", and in the intervals of risking their lives, some priests engaged in hunting, billiards, or worse.

The orthodox Catholics were leaderless because most of their bishops had emigrated. Only seven had remained in France, and of these only one, Moreau of Mâcon, stayed in his episcopal town. And in any case they were all marked men. It was out of the question for them to resume the direction of their old dioceses though M. de Maillé La Tour Landry, Bishop of Saint-Papoul, a tough ex-soldier, from May 1795 was ordaining candidates for the ministry who came to him in Paris. The *abbé* Bernet, in later years when he was a bishop himself, would tell the romantic story of his ordination by Mgr de Saint-Papoul: "*Trouvez-vous ce soir à minuit, rue des Rats.*" Of the émigré prelates, two (the bishops of Vienne and of Vaison) heroically returned to France in 1797; two others came back in 1799. The rest continued to attempt to exercise their authority from lodging-houses or the antechambers of the great in Germany and England, or from monasteries in Spain. In theory Vicars-General (like Linsolas at Lyon, Meilloc at Angers, and Papillant at Rouen) who had stayed behind in hiding gave directions to the faithful clergy on their bishops' behalf. In practice it was difficult and dangerous to get in touch with the clergy or to communicate regularly with the bishop, while episcopal rulings, when they came, tended to be rigoristic, unrealistic, and out-of-date. When one of the old bishops died, three or more canons of the cathedral would meet in secret to appoint a capitular vicar to administer the diocese; or, since the procedures of the *ancien régime* seemed, to some, inappropriate in pagan France, application to the Pope for an apostolic administrator would be made. Inevitably, there were delays and confusions. At Lyon, after Marbeuf's death in April 1799, such canons of the old chapter as could be found in the diocese named one of their own number as adminis-trator, while the Papal Congregation for the affairs of France named one of the old bishop's companions, who received the support of Linsolas, the rigorists in France, and of Louis XVIII in exile. To M. Emery's despair the émigrés and rigorists prevailed.

The orthodox received no leadership from Rome; indeed, what leadership could Rome have given until a government arose in France which was willing to negotiate? That there had been a possibility of a settlement in the summer of 1796 was soon forgotten—except by Bonaparte. On 28 December 1797 a corporal of the pontifical guard assassinated General Duphot, the young hero of the army of Italy. Two months later General Berthier marched in and proclaimed a Roman Republic from the Capitol, with depressingly predictable rhetoric about Cato, Pompey, Brutus, and Cicero—who could have guessed that the day of Caesar was so near at hand? Pius VI became a prisoner. He was moved to France and at Valence he died in captivity on 12 fructidor year VII (29 August 1799). Citizen Chauveau, municipal officer of the commune, recorded the decease of "Jean Ange Braschi, exer-cising the profession of pontiff". There were those who asked whether anyone would exercise that profession again.

14. The Twilight of the Revolutionary Cults

Births, marriages, and deaths were drably commemorated in the Republic which "did not recognize or pay for any religion". New-born children, La Revellière-Lépaux complained, were carried off to an office to be registered like packages for the customs, and the dead were hygienically rushed away with a minimum of fuss; the romance of marriage palled as the couple pushed their way to the registry, "obstructed by a horde of crude persons, whose disgusting remarks and cynical gestures would wound the least sensitive of men"; once inside, they were crowded onto dirty tavern benches under an ugly statue of Hymen until the clerks behind the registers had time to pronounce them man and wife by noting down the particulars. The legislators were no longer backing a deistical cult as a substitute for Christianity, but there was public demand for ceremonies to dignify the crude events of the *état civil*. Poets—Fontanes, Richer de Sérizy, and Legouvé—became preoccupied with tombs, with the failure of the nation to reverence the last resting-places of its dead. The law forbids priests to process to the graveside, Legouvé told the Institut in October 1797, but families ought to do so.

> La sensibilité n'est pas le fanatisme,
> De la religion gardons l'humanité.

There was, too, the question that dominated the intellectual speculation of the day, that of teaching, encouraging, and enforcing morality. "A good catechism of morality", said the journal, the *Décade,* on 30 messidor year VI, "is the crowning achievement of philosophy". In two successive years, the

Institut set for its prize essay competition the title, *Quelles sont les institutions les plus propres à fonder la morale d'un peuple?* But before the prize was offered, the heirs of the eighteenth-century *philosophes* were devising austere proposals. In a three-volume treatise, *L'Origine de tous les cultes* (1794), Dupuis, a disciple of Voltaire, claimed to have "cast the anchor of truth in the midst of the Ocean of Time". Mithra, Adonis, Osiris, Christ, and all other cult figures were "solar myths" and, since "nothing justifies imposture", religion must be abandoned and men must face the fact that the only instruments they have to encourage morality are "good laws". The year after Dupuis' ponderous argument appeared, the Republic published Condorcet's *Esquisse d'un tableau historique du progrès de l'espirit humain,* the famous forecast of indefinite progress for mankind. Here was a lofty inspiration for moral conduct, though a dangerous one, for intermediate consequences were to be ignored, "except in so far as they eventually influence the greater mass of the human race"—an encouragement to that vague utopian invocation of posterity which had been used to gild the guillotine, on which Condorcet himself had perished. At eighty-six years of age Saint-Lambert, one of the familiars of the authentic *philosophes* of the mid-eighteenth century, found Condorcet's vista of the future unhelpful; he was optimistic, however, about human nature, which made his *Principes des mœurs chez toutes les nations* (1798) cheerful reading. He argued that the mechanisms of pleasure, pain, and fear that God has implanted in us make it impossible for us to find our own happiness without seeking that of our fellows. From this comfortable assurance, a series of moral exhortations flowed. One of these went well beyond the demands of Christian charity: "Pay your taxes with joy; you could not make a better use of your money". Sylvain Maréchal drew the moral from this astonishing faith in humanity. At the beginning of year VI he published a proposal for a humanist Church, with an atheistical creed and a special hymn to proclaim the disinterested nature of moral conduct:

> A man is a vile and despicable clod
> Whose benevolence needs the existence of God;
> My sole God is virtue.

More serious philosophers had less confidence in human nature. With the "Idéologues", who made the Institut their fortress and the *Décade* their mouth-piece, the sensationalist philosophy of Condillac was taken to extremes. Sensation became the source of all understanding; it was not a case of "I think, therefore I am", but of existing and thinking being the same thing. Cabanis was willing to concede that human awareness would flow on to lose itself in the principle of life that lies behind all things, but this "God" was no more relevant to human affairs than he was in the universe of Laplace's *Traité de mécanique céleste* (1799). Man had no soul, no separate identity after death; his moral promptings were but a confused sensibility bound up with organic, visceral existence. In a work with a fashionable title, *Quels sont les moyens de fonder la morale chez un peuple* (1798), Destutt de Tracy summarized the conclusions of the Idéologues about practical conduct: justice was simply social convention, to be virtuous was to confine the desires to the resources one found within oneself, and morality became an unobtrusive, stoical conformity.

It was a doctrine reflecting the disillusionment of the revolutionary generation. Saint-Lambert's confidence in human nature was disproved by the conduct of the rich in post-thermidorian France. Condorcet's lyrical prophecies were unconvincing to men who had seen the destructive possibilities of enthusiasm. That other prop of the idea of a lay morality, the emulation of the patriotic virtues of classical antiquity, was also out of favour; the tragedies of Sophocles, said Volney (who had once extolled the Ancients) were as crude in their fatalism as the beliefs of the Red Indians, and the Romans had conducted themselves as barbarously as the Huns. There was disillusionment too about the capacity of the mass of mankind for rational and unselfish action. In a famous discourse on

12 floréal year V, La Revellière-Lépaux said that only the educated man could practise the social virtues by rational choice—"*cela n'est pas vrai d'un peuple*". The stock argument of eighteenth-century Christian apologists, that religion was a social necessity, was as popular as ever; indeed the Revolution had reinforced it—except that Catholicism, or even Christianity, was not necessarily the religion that was required. La Revellière thought the multitude incapable of acting morally without a belief in God and the immortality of the soul. Without these two dogmas, said the handbook to the most important of the new religions invented after Thermidor, men would be "but ravening wolves".

Since a religion was necessary, someone had to work out the details. In propitious times credal and liturgical invention must be an interesting hobby. For his "Culte des Adorateurs", Daubermesnil studied the writings of Rousseau, the paintings of Greuze, the stern facades of Pompeii, and the sensuous ornamentation of Indian temples; his priests, annually elected officials, would tend an eternal fire at an altar set in spacious gardens; at funerals they would burn incense and pour libations of milk, honey, and wine. Doctor Bressy, for his version of natural religion, wished to have scientists and medical men (such as himself) serving as priests, and recommended laboratory experiments to impress the vulgar in place of a liturgy. Others proposed committees of wise old men who would conflate into a single moral code the precepts of Moses and Christ, Confucius and Mahomet. More seriously there were those who saw the possibility of using religion to propagate the ideal of social equality which the Revolution had abandoned; at Sens, Benoist-Lamothe, an ex-noble and a communistic disciple of Mably, preached a *culte social*, while in Paris, at the beginning of 1796, the new sect of the "Panthéonistes" was promoted by a communistic group, the "Égaux", soon to become famous in history by their conspiracy against the Directory.

The most serious of the new religions, and the only one to become influential, was "Théophilanthropie". Both Daubermesnil and Benoist-Lamothe eventually joined it; so too did La Revellière, one of the Directors, Dupont de Nemours the economist, Bernardin de Saint-Pierre the romantic writer, M.-J. Chénier the poet, and Sébastien Mercier the journalist. Clearly the new cult had an appeal both to men of imagination and to realists. In September 1796 the bookseller Chemin published a *Manuel des Théoanthrophiles* (later changed to *Manuel des Théophilanthropes*). The dogmas proclaimed were those of the cult of the Être Suprême, God and the immortality of the soul. Without these beliefs men would cheerfully do evil, believing that "their crimes would be buried for ever with them in the tomb". The Doctrine of Original Sin was explicitly denied: "I do not ask the power to do the good; Thou hast given me this power, and with it the conscience to love the good, reason to know it, and liberty to choose it". So much for St Paul. In so far as the theology of the revolutionary cults is worth studying, here is the decisive point of challenge to Christianity, as Christianity was then understood. The argument was put with its full emotional content by Benoist-Lamothe, in his hymn for the Theophilanthropic church at Sens:

> Merciful God, thy suppliant people seek
> Protection for the mother and the child,
> Thou couldst not strike an infant for the sake
> Of imagined crimes imputed to the weak.

The value of the protest, during the eighteenth and nineteenth centuries, by *philosophes,* deists, and agnostics against sub-Christian ideas of God held by Christians themselves, has never been adequately acknowledged by churchmen. A Christian today would agree with Benoist-Lamothe's hymn, rather than with an orthodox sermon on Original Sin by an eighteenth-century divine.

The publication of the *Manuel* brought Chemin to public notice and drew to him an ally, Valentin Haüy, who had founded a choir of blind singers in the church of Saint-Eustache five years before the Revolution. The choir still existed, having found employment in the revolutionary fêtes, and Haüy brought it to lead the singing in the services of Theophilanthropy. The eloquent public support of La Revellière, subventions from the police funds, and hints that government jobs might become available to faithful attenders helped the new cult along, as well as its own merits. By the end of the winter of year VI it had sixteen places of worship in Paris. In the provinces, Theophilanthropy caught on in certain towns, mostly in central France, where the de-Christianization movement had been strongest; in the Yonne it spread to rural areas as well, but this was unusual. Its leaders had often been active in the earlier revolutionary cults. At Versailles, Bourges, Bordeaux, Châlons-sur-Marne, Rouen, Auxerre, the directors of the Theophilanthropic observances were ex-priests, now administrative officials, masters in government schools, and newspaper editors; elsewhere, we find former ecclesiastics volunteering sermons. One preached a discourse on the immortality of the soul which, under the *ancien régime,* he had dedicated to the Bishop of Coutances. These men, we may believe, were rediscovering what remained of their original vocation for, unlike the cults of Reason and the Supreme Being, Theophilanthropy did not set itself up as hostile to Christianity, or even as its replacement. It was the "minimum" religion, which tolerated those who were prepared to take the venture of belief still further. At Sens, Benoist-Lamothe even claimed for his group the title of "Christians":

> We believe that Jesus was sent to earth
> To instruct and guide us;
> I swear to remain faithful
> To his sacred gospel.

Theophilanthropy was not a creation of popular enthusiasm. It was an emenity, provided by a few experts and enthusiasts, which was taken up by only a limited clientele. Its spread was dependent upon the accidents of local leadership and eloquence. It was strong at Paris, where Siauve, an ex-*curé,* edited its newspaper and where intellectual preachers abounded, and at Auxerre, where another ex-*curé*, Chaisneau, and two former priests, all members of the municipal administration, provided expertise and authority. By contrast, at Château-Thiery, under an illiterate schoolmaster with the improbable name of Rubarbe, there was no progress. Though in some places local administrators combined the official ceremonies of the *décadi* with the new liturgy, the Directory refused to make Theophilanthropy the established faith. Ironical replies from his fellow Directors greeted La Revellière's proposal of a State religion; Barras suggested that it was his duty to get himself executed to provide the new cult with a martyrdom to build on, and Carnot declared that absurdity and unintelligibility were the essence of a successful creed and that in these respects nothing could hope to compete with Catholicism. After 22 floréal year VI (11 May 1798), when the Directory took measures against the "Jacobins", the extreme political left, governmental support was withdrawn from Theophilanthropy altogether. Anticlericals suspected that the lectors of the new Church, officiating in blue robes, were fostering a revival of priestcraft, while the scoffers who had found entertainment in the outrages of the de-Christianization, now joined the Catholics in finding the new religion ridiculous.

So Theophilanthropy faded. Of the two great inspirations of the revolutionary cults, one had reached its term. Deism, however numerous its intellectual following, had failed to find embodiment in institutional form. The other inspiration, patriotism, remained, and to this the Directory now turned. Henceforward it was content to enforce the ceremonies of the *décadi*. Municipal officials were ordered to attend to read the laws, all marriages were to be celebrated there, and the names of soldiers fallen in battle were to be solemnly commemorated. There were signs of diligence in these observances in Paris, in the central anticlerical department of the Yonne, and on the eastern frontier, but after the summer of 1799 these died away. In the battered churches, only unwilling officials, recalcitrant children, impatient marriage parties, and stray dogs turned up to hear the reading of the *Bulletin* and perfunctory martial music. When Bonaparte took over, he instructed the prefects to leave the laws unenforced and to allow the whole boring routine to fall into disuse.

Before it failed, Theophilanthropy had reminded men of the old argument that religion is the surest guarantee of popular morality; the *décadi,* as it foundered, revealed the usefulness of an established Church to dignify the public ceremonies necessary to State and family life. The revolutionary cults which had arisen to replace Catholicism finished up by exemplifying the most cogent political arguments for its restoration.

15. Towards the Concordat

After the event, all roads seemed to lead to Bonaparte. Brumaire was distinguished from the other political and military coups of the Revolution by the realism with which the chief conspirator knotted together the minimum, ineluctable, conflicting demands of varying groups of Frenchmen into a stable settlement—acting so swiftly and so surely that Jacobin contemporaries and republican historians after them have never succeeded in providing that prerequisite for a critical assessment, a convincing picture of how things could have been otherwise.

The nexus of the settlement was the Concordat with the Catholic Church. Bonaparte's own religion, a blend of sentimental memories and the soldier's fatalism, was real, but was only incidentally involved in his decision to negotiate with Rome. At the age of seventeen he had written an essay in support of Rousseau's condemnation of "pure Christianity" as a menace to the State, going outside Rousseau's brief to complain that excessive fidelity to the Gospels encourages subjects to criticize their sovereign. Fourteen years later, himself the ruler of a State, he negotiated with the Church simply as an institution with power over the minds of men. His object was to harness this power to the service of his rule. "The people must have a religion; this religion must be in the control of the government." "Society cannot exist without inequality of fortunes", and, without a belief in a future life, the poor would not accept their lot. If a respectable cult is not provided, the multitude will resort to some nauseating substitute: "religion is a sort of inoculation . . . which, by satisfying our love of the marvellous, makes us immune to charlatans and sorcerers."

As a technician in revolutionary expansionism, it was obvious to Bonaparte that anticlericalism was not for export. This lesson he had learned while campaigning in Italy, and he knew it applied equally to Belgium and the Rhineland. Some show of religion would be useful in foreign policy—"if I had not believed in God, who would have been willing to negotiate with me?" Spain and Austria might incline towards a Catholic France, and after Marengo the First Consul wrote to the Emperor of Austria urging him to turn his arms against the English, Prussians, or Muscovites, all "further from the Church". The soldiers and officials of the Revolution had grown accustomed to speaking of the Pope with contempt. They were the heirs of the Gallican tradition and of a decade of revolutionary libel and innuendo; besides, they had marched into the papal capital and had seen its poverty-stricken populace, its comic-opera soldiers, and cows grazing in the Forum. But to Bonaparte (who, incidentally, never saw the Eternal City), the Pope's power was not to be measured by popular prejudices or the contemptible details of an ill-ruled principality. One of his earliest decrees as First Consul (30 December 1799) prescribed funeral honours for Pius VI, who had died in captivity at Valence—"a man who had occupied one of the greatest offices in the world". The Pope, as Bonaparte was accustomed to say, was a "lever of opinion", a moral force, whimsically assessed in military terms as equivalent to a "corps of 200,000 men".

A corps of something like half that strength would in practical effect be immediately released by a pacification in the Vendée. The brutal guerilla war in the West still continued. General Hoche had told the Directory that only a religious settlement could end it. General Hédouville went under flag of truce to see the *abbé* Bernier, former *curé* of Saint-Laud of Angers and now the director of the rebels' councils. All the way on his journey Hédouville saw that men and women working the fields were signalling his passage, civilian irregulars ready to strike if the word was given. "We must begin", he reported, "by protecting the free exercise of

religion and its exterior ceremonies". Bernier came to Paris
and dined with the First Consul on 26 January 1800. In the
following September he was summoned to act as the government's representative in the negotiations for the Concordat—
to please the Vendéans, and to show them that their sacrifices
had not been in vain. "It was by making myself a Catholic",
said Bonaparte, "that I finished the war of the Vendée".

An army commander leading peasant conscripts knew what
would satisfy the mass of the French population better than
the politicians in Paris. It was a commonplace among the
soldiers that rural France was weary of urban iconoclasm.
"Our religious revolution is a failure", General Clarke had
reported to Bonaparte in Italy, "people have become Roman
Catholic again . . . maybe we are at the point when we need
the Pope to bring to the Revolution the support of the priests,
and by consequence of the countryside, which they have
succeeded in dominating once more". The de-Christianizers
were discredited, the revolutionary religions, which had never
taken root in the countryside, had now withered in the towns.
If a religion was to be found to bind together society by
providing those standard benefits that were generally agreed
to be necessary, a basis for morality and decent ceremonies
for State and family occasions, it would have to be the
traditional religion of France, Catholicism. In this sense, the
restoration of the altars would be the wish of the nation. "My
policy is to govern men as the majority wish to be governed.
That is the way, I believe, in which one recognizes the
sovereignty of the people. . . . If I ruled a people of Jews, I'd
rebuild the Temple of Solomon." In moving towards the
Concordat Bonaparte was fulfilling the unspoken wishes of the
mass of Frenchmen.

But he also knew that limitations were imposed on him by
the same unformed, obscure instincts of public opinion to
which he was responding. The liberal and egalitarian achievements of the Revolution could not be abandoned. Roman
Catholicism could not be described as the "dominant" religion:
the Concordat was to go no further than admitting that it

was the religion of "the majority of French citizens". Toleration, civil marriage, and divorce must be preserved. The
Gallican liberties were sacrosanct; that is why the "Organic
Articles" were to be fraudulently added to the Concordat
under the pretext that they were merely "police regulations".
The Constitutional Church would be wound up, but the early,
idealistic days of the Revolution must not be called in question
by submitting its clergy to open humiliation. And, above all,
the buyers of Church property had to be guaranteed for ever
in the possession of their gains.

These were the frontiers of manœuvre. Facing such complexities and obstacles a less intelligent, a less ruthless statesman than Bonaparte would have failed. His brusque, vulgarian
conduct of the negotiations should not deceive us. Behind the
bullying, a first-class diplomatic mind was at work. "If
there was an art at which Napoleon excelled", wrote Pasquier,
"it was that of balancing all interests and of combining the
measure of satisfaction which must be granted to each". The
Concordat was the supreme example of his genius for syn-
thetic conciliation.

Before discussions with Rome began, the basis of a compromise was clear in his mind. After the battle of Marengo he
put three points to Cardinal Martiniana: the Church to be
restored with a new episcopate, the State to pay clerical
salaries, and churchmen to renounce all claim to their former
properties. "Go to Rome", he said, "and tell the Holy Father
that the First Consul wishes to make him a gift of thirty
million Frenchmen". The Concordat that was ratified more
than a year later was incomplete and equivocal. Nothing was
said about vicars-general, professors of seminaries, monks and
nuns, about chapters, bishops' palaces, and the presbyteries of
curés; the salaries of most of the clergy were not covered; the
"police regulations" referred to might be (and were) intolerable
to Rome; Pope and First Consul could have disagreed
ruinously about the latter's nominations to bishoprics, or
about the revision of the boundaries of dioceses and parishes.
But the weaknesses of the Concordat, considered as a theoret-

ical exercise in draughtsmanship, were to contribute to its
strength as a realistic act of statesmanship. The three principles laid down to Cardinal Martiniana were guaranteed;
for the rest, the Pope, the Catholics of France, and Bonaparte
himself were agreeing to work together, while retaining their
own divergent hopes about what the future would bring. The
oath which the clergy had to take was extreme, in that it included the obligation to inform the secular authorities of
activities prejudicial to the State. Yet it was sound by the
principles of casuistry: it was not imposing acceptance of the
"Constitution", or the "laws", or principles or ideas, but
simply of the Government. The Civil Constitution of the
Clergy, comprehensive, logical, legalistic, precise down to the
details of salaries, presented to the Church on a take-it-or-
leave-it basis, and enforced by an oath which obscured the
issues of loyalty involved, was a disaster. The Concordat, the
bare bones of an agreement, riddled with omissions and
occasions for dispute, embodying a ruthless but unambiguous
and limited oath, and squarely negotiated with ecclesiastical
authority, worked.

The arguments for the Concordat that were eventually put
to the Assemblies by the government orators were of Bonaparte's kind, exclusively social, the truth or falsehood of
religion being "a purely theological question which does not
concern us". But the survival of the Church to become once
again an establishment had been ensured by the devotion of
the minority of Christians who were passionately convinced
of the truth of their beliefs, of the "purely theological
question" which did not concern the government. Their
fortitude in persecution and determination to resume the
public exercise of their religion as soon as the law permitted
had won back the opinion of the majority to favour the
restoration of an official, nominal Christianity. Councillors
of State, sent on tours of the Departments on the eve of the
Concordat, reluctantly conceded that there was no alternative
to a restoration of the altars; though, one observed sardonically, the people "would rather have their bells back

without priests than the priests without bells". One way or another the majority of children receiving education in France were being taught by ecclesiastics. The Frères des Écoles Chrétiennes had reopened schools in forty towns. A report from Paris said that children of deputies and generals were being educated by "fanatics", and that raging anticlericals of 1792 and 1793 "did not regard their daughters as well brought up if they had not made their first communion". Another despatch from the Manche said the people preferred to pay for clerical education, "hoping to get better instruction and purer morals"; another from the Rhone-Alps area said "the old *curés* and *vicaires* teach children to read, the former nuns maintain schools for girls; in this respect the old régime is back again". The teaching orders of nuns were active in various towns, often at the invitation of the departmental administrators. The government was even more anxious to get the female religious back to run the hospitals; in December 1800 the Minister of the Interior allowed the Filles de la Charité de Saint-Vincent de Paul to recruit again, with official financial help, and the ladies of Saint-Thomas de Villeneuve were soon allowed to reopen their orphanages.

This was the state of opinion in France while negotiations for the Concordat were proceeding. And it was evident that the tide of intellectual fashion (whether following opinion or leading it) was flowing towards Catholicism. Outside one or two *salons*, the Idéologues had little influence and their predecessors the *philosophes* were universally decried. The literature of dissidence of the eighteenth century was suspect now as elevating the rights of man as an individual, but forgetting his social duties. Behind its brilliant phrases, said Bonald, the mentality of terrorism had lurked, like plague in a precious cargo from the Levant. It is true that Bonald's onslaught on the *philosophes* (1796) had not been widely distributed (though Bonaparte had read it with approval while campaigning in Egypt), and that the *abbé* Barruel's hysterical theories of intellectual conspiracies were more credible to *émigrés* than to those who had lived through the confusions he systematized. It was, rather, La Harpe's lectures on fanaticism, delivered at the *lycée* of Paris in 1797, which set the new fashion—facile denunciations which could only have impressed the public because they provided a message that it was anxious to hear. In the same year Rivarol published his *Discours sur l'homme intellectuel et moral*. "The radical defect of philosophy", he said, "is that it cannot speak to the heart. . . . Even if we consider religions as nothing more than organized superstitions, they would still be beneficial to the human race; for in the heart of man there is a religious fibre that nothing can extirpate". Fontanes, always moving with the current, now proclaimed his transfer of allegiance from Voltaire to Racine and the Christian seventeenth century; then, a proscript of Fructidor, he fled to England, where under old elm trees and in country inns he told Chateaubriand the story of La Harpe's conversion and of the growing hatred of *philosophaillerie*. Ballanche, embittered against the Revolution by the memory of the destruction of Lyon, meditated upon the civilizing force of the emotions, a preservative against the cold despair that reason brings. Everyone was saying now that morality needed sentiment, more especially religious sentiment, as its basis. Since war and inflation continued to corrupt society, writers remained obsessed with the problem of devising sanctions for conduct, and in April 1800 (in *De la littérature*), Mme de Stael added to the debate the thought that "scientific progress makes moral progress a necessity". She was in tune with the times too when she lifted the *philosophes*' censures on the "Gothic" Middle Ages and praised Christianity for teaching equality, the sanctity of marriage, and chivalry to a barbarous world.

The arguments were accumulating for Chateaubriand (whose *Génie du Christianisme* was to be in the shops four days before Easter Sunday 1802, when a solemn Te Deum was sung in Notre-Dame to celebrate the Concordat). In Chateaubriand's masterpiece of apologetics, subtle rhythms and haunting evocative writing are sometimes used to decorate the unspiritual, calculating arguments that were characteristic of the age and its attitude towards religion. Yet his eloquence is also used to convey an inspiring impression of the heroism and selflessness of so many Christians during the revolutionary persecutions. In so far as there was a religious revival in France, as distinct from the official "restoration of the altars", here was its source and inspiration. Chateaubriand emphasizes that the dynamic of Christianity comes from its claim to face suffering and death and transform them, while to Deism these grim accidents only serve to call in question the goodness of God. "O Nature, sweet and good, eternal mother of us all", says the *philosophe*, ridiculously, perched on the edge of the crater of a raging volcano—a dramatic incident in a satire written by a citizen of Saint-Malo and his two nephews during the Terror. By contrast, their allegiance turned to those who faced the realities of suffering. "I saw priests mounting the scaffold", said the elder nephew later, after his own ordination, "and this spectacle implanted in my mind my priestly vocation"—a vocation to which he was to bring his younger and more famous brother, Félicité de Lamennais.

"If Rome understands her position truly", wrote Chateaubriand in the *Génie*, "she never had before her such great hopes, such a brilliant destiny. We say hopes, for we count tribulations in the number of things that the Church of Jesus Christ desires". These words were prophetic. Yet two years earlier, at the Conclave of Venice, the Papacy had seemed on the verge of disolution. But fortunately for the Church the long fifteen weeks of intrigue in the freezing, smoky chapel of the monastery of St George did not lead to the election of an Austrian nominee, or a rigorist of the Zelanti party. Instead, the ballots of the cardinals at last fell upon Chiaramonti, Bishop of Imola. The new Pope, Pius VII, has sometimes been misjudged in the light of his famous Christmas homily of 1797: "the democratic form adopted amongst us . . . is not repugnant to the Gospels." These words should not be taken out of context. In fact, the sermon went on to say that democracy "demands sublime virtues" which could only be nurtured by Christianity; the general effect was to recognize the Cisalpine Republic as the *de facto* government, but to make the blood of republicans run cold with the thought that only great Christian virtues could save them. It is a mistake to say that the new Pope sympathized with the ideals of the Revolution or that he was a sycophant of power. He had simply learnt the lesson of the revolutionary age, the lesson that Emery was teaching in France: that Christianity must be able to live with a *de facto* government, whatever its nature.

In the light of this belief, undeterred by the embittered clamour of the French royalists and the doubts of his own entourage, Pius VII came to an agreement with Bonaparte. Leadership was thrust upon him, for no other voice could speak for the Church of France. Most of the surviving orthodox bishops were in exile where, with a few exceptions, they were forgetting nothing and learning nothing. M. Emery approved of the promise laid down by the decree of nivôse (28 December 1799) and got Bonaparte to rule (against Fouché, his Minister of Police) that émigrés and deportees were fully entitled to take it and return. On the other hand Cardinal de la Rochefoucauld, who had held the archiepiscopal see of Rouen under the *ancien régime,* declared that those who made the promise were "taking the equivalent of all the oaths of the Revolution". In one form of words or another all but fifteen of the exiled bishops, out of touch with France and with reality, followed this line. As for the Constitutional Church, it struggled on, though the reports of the councillors of state sent round the departments were practically unanimous in declaring that its influence had collapsed. It held its last Council in Paris in 1801; this gathering went on until August, when Fouché ordered its deputies to go home lest their presence offended the eyes of the Cardinal Legate coming to negotiate the Concordat. In any case the First Consul could not have initiated discussions with one branch of the French Church without making any approach to the other impossible. His plan was to get rid of both hierarchies and to nominate a new episcopate. For this, the Pope was indispensible, both to obtain the resignation of the orthodox bishops (or to dismiss them) and to approve the nomination of new ones.

Ten years before, the National Assembly had ostentatiously ignored the Pope while devising the Civil Constitution of the Clergy: now, the restoration of the French Church was brought about by an agreement with the Pope alone. Of all ecclesiastical institutions it was the Papacy which gained as a result of the Revolution. Alone Pius VII negotiated terms for the once proud and independent Gallican Church. With the concurrence of the Government he summoned its bishops to resign and deposed the thirty-eight who refused to obey. Then, when Napoleon turned to persecute him, he bore himself nobly in adversity, humbly and sympathetically intransigent. Yet, when the man himself has been given full credit for politic insight and saintliness of character, the real reasons for the enormous increase in the prestige of the Papacy are seen to lie deeper. The Revolution had swept away the kings of France with their Gallican traditions and the Enlightened Despots who organized their cardinals to elect weaklings to the Chair of Peter; it had overturned the ecclesiastical prince-doms of Germany, the exclusively noble episcopate of France, and the whole proud, vested, aristocratic interest that had battened on the Church; it had broken the claims of secular sovereigns and quasi-independent missionary orders to direct the work of Catholic missions overseas. Catholicism was to reknit its fibres, not along the old traditional patterns of the erastian national Churches, but with the Pope as its centre. Among the politic bishops the Gallican spirit was to remain alive, but the lower clergy would become more and more ultramontane, looking to Rome for guidance, and overseas missions were to revive under the direction of the Roman Propaganda.

But all this lay in the future. The negotiations for the Concordat began in November 1800 and, after alarms and vicissitudes, ratifications were exchanged by September 1801 and all was ready for publication by Easter of the following year. The details of the agreement, the shifts and heart-burnings which accompanied the establishment of the new Concordatory Church, the subsequent stormy relations of Pope and Emperor and the role of the Concordat in French history throughout the next century do not now concern us. We leave France under its First Consul preparing for the great Easter ceremony in Notre-Dame; a nation bitterly divided by memories of the war that had raged between the Revolution and the Church; the generals cursing the whole business of reconciling Church and State as a fraud and a *"capucinade"*; brand-new copies of the *Génie du Christianisme* on the drawing-room tables of polite society; the Vendée at peace and Bernier looking forward to his bishopric; Archbishop Boisgelin conning his sermon notes, for he was to preach at the ceremonies at Notre-Dame as he had preached at the coronation of Louis XVI, twenty-seven years ago; the bells all ringing, and the purchasers of Church property snug at their firesides, secure at last in possession of their gains.

A Note on Books

A General Histories of the Catholic Church in France in the Revolutionary period

P. de la Gorce, *Histoire religieuse de la Révolution française*, 5 vols, 1902-23. Excellent narrative; strong Catholic bias.

C. Ledré, *L'Église de France sous la Révolution*, 1949.

A. Dansette, *Religious History of Modern France*, 2 vols, 1961; an English translation, abridged, of the French work published in 1948.

* A. Latreille, *L'Église catholique et la Révolution française*, 2 vols, 1946-50. Still the best history.

* E. Préclin & E. Jarry, *Les luttes doctrinales et politiques aux XVIIe et XVIIIe siècles*, 2 vols, 1955-6, being vol. XIX of the *Histoire de l'Église*, ed. Fliche & Martin.

* J. Leflon, *La crise révolutionnaire*, 1949, being vol. XX of the Fliche & Martin series.

* D. Rops, *L'Église des Révolutions*, 1960, being vol. IX of the author's *Histoire de l'Église du Christ*.

A. Latreille, R. Rémond et al., *Histoire du Catholicisme en France*, vol. III, 1962.

B Towards a full Bibliography

Extensive bibliographies are found in the four general histories marked with an asterisk above. The most convenient way to add to them and bring them up to date is to use the book reviews in the following periodicals.

1. *Annales historiques de la Révolution française.*

2. *Revue de l'histoire de l'Église de France* (which, in addition to reviews, lists all the relevant articles in learned journals and local periodicals).

3. *Revue d'histoire ecclésiastique* (Louvain).

One must remember that all the general histories of the Revolution and many of the monographs and articles concerning it are relevant to our subject. For further reading on matters concerning education, see the books referred to in L. Grimaud, *Histoire de la liberté d'enseignement en France,* vols. I & II, 1944. To these add M. Gontard, *L'Enseignement primaire en France* (1958). For the mass of writing on the history of ideas, see the reviews in the *Revue d'histoire littéraire de la France* and the bibliography of J. Kitchin's *La Décade (1794-1807): un journal philosophique,* (1965).

On methodological questions, Gabriel Le Bras, *Études de sociologie religieuse* 2 vols, 1955-6, should be consulted. On the de-Christianization movement, see the bibliography of Richard Cobb's monumental work *Les armées révolutionnaires: instrument de la Terreur dans les départements,* 2 vols, 1961-3 —a book which has entirely renewed our approach to this difficult subject.

For the Protestants (referred to only incidentally in this study), E. G. Léonard is the best authority (see his *Le Protestant français,* 1953).

B. C. Poland's *French Protestantism and the Revolution* (1957) is useful but must be read in the light of the criticisms of D. Robert, *Les Églises réformées en France, 1800–1830* 1961.

C *A Short List of Fifty Books*

In addition to the titles already mentioned, the following are added to provide a short reading list of fifty items altogether. The choice is necessarily unbalanced, partly by the compiler's prejudices and limitations, partly by the inevitable exclusion of references to original sources, general works on the Revolution, and (with a few exceptions) of articles. It has also proved impossible to give a fair idea of the vast literature on the Church of the *ancien régime* and on the movements of ideas in the eighteenth century.

1. ANCIEN RÉGIME

E. Préclin, *Les Jansénistes du XVIII siècle et la Constitution civile du clergé*, 1929.

M. L. Fracart, *La fin de l'ancien régime à Niort*, 1956.

P. Chevallier, *Loménie de Brienne et l'ordre monastique, 1766–1789*, 2 vols, 1960.

J. McManners, *French Ecclesiastical Society under the Ancien Régime: a Study of Angers*, 1960.

A. Schaer, *Le Clergé paroissial catholique en haute Alsace sous l'ancien régime, 1648-1789*, 1966.

2. THE MOVEMENT OF IDEAS

R. R. Palmer, *Catholics and Unbelievers in 18th-century France*, 1939.

Lester G. Crocker, *Nature & Culture: Ethical Thought in the French Enlightenment*, 1963.

D. Mornet, *Les origines intellectuelles de la Révolution française* (1932)—a famous thesis, now under attack on methodological grounds (see F. Furet and A. Dupront (eds.) *Livre et societé dans la France du 18ᵉ siècle* (1965) espec. pp. 213–33).

A. Monod, *Les défenseurs français du Christianisme de 1670 à 1802*, 1916.

F. Picavet, *Les Idéologues*, 1890.

R. Fargher, "The Retreat from Voltaireanism, 1800-1815" in *The French Mind*, ed. W. Moore, R. Sutherland and E. Starkie, 1952.

3. GENERAL

A. Mathiez, *Contributions à l'histoire religieuse de la Révolution* 1907; *La Révolution et l'Église*, 1910; *Rome et le clergé français sous la Constituante*, 1911.

A. Aulard, *Le Christianisme et la Révolution française*, 1924.

A. Sicard, *Le clergé de France pendant la Révolution*, 3 vols, 1912-17.

Dom H. Leclercq, *L'Église constitutionnelle*, 1934.
S. Delacroix, *La réorganisation de l'Église de France après la Révolution, 1801-9* I, 1962.

4. AREA STUDIES

P. Pisani, *L'Église de Paris et la Révolution*, 4 vols, 1910-11.

E. Sévèstre, *La vie religieuse dans les principales villes normandes pendant la Révolution* I, 1945.

Marquis de Roux, *Histoire religieuse de la Révolution à Poitiers et dans la Vienne*, 1952.

F. Bridoux, *Histoire religieuse du départment de la Seine-et-Marne pendant la Révolution* 2 vols, 1953.

J. Plumet, *L'Évêché de Tournai pendant la Révolution française*, 1963.

J. Eich, *Histoire religieuse du département de la Moselle pendant la Révolution*, I, 1964.

M. Faucheux, *L'Insurrection vendéenne de 1793, aspects économiques et Sociaux*, 1964.

5. BIOGRAPHIES AND STUDIES OF GROUPS

J. Leflon, *M. Emery*, 2 vols, 1944-7; *Etienne-Alexandre Bernier*, 2 vols, 1958; *Pie VII* 1958; *Nicolas Philbert, évêque constitutionnel des Ardennes*, 1954.

C. Ledré, *Le culte caché sous la Révolution: les missions de l'abbé Linsolas* (n.d.).

E. Lavaquary, *Le cardinal de Boisgelin*, 2 vols, 1920.

M. G. Hutt, "The Role of the Curés in the Estates General", *Journal of Ecclesiastical History* VI, 1955; "The Curés and the Third Estate", ibid., VIII, 1957.

B. Rigault, *Histoire générale de l'Institut des Frères des Écoles chrétiennes*, III, 1940.

J. Boussoulade, *Moniales et hospitalières dans la tourmente révolutionnaire: Les communautés religieuses de l'ancien diocèse de Paris,* 1962.

B. Plongeron, *Les réguliers de Paris devant le serment constitutionnel,* 1964—important use of statistical method. See also Plongeron's "Regards sur l'historiographie religieuse de la Révolution I, les serments", *A.h.R.F.,* 1967, with other articles to follow.

6. DE-CHRISTIANIZATION AND THE REVOLUTIONARY CULTS

A. Mathiez, *L'origine des cultes révolutionnaires,* 1904; *La Théophilanthropie et le culte décadaire,* 1903.

A. Aulard, *Le culte de la Raison et de l'Être suprême,* 1892.

P. Trahard, *La sensibilité révolutionaire, 1789–94,* 1936.

M. L Dowd, *Pageant-master of the Republic: Jacques-Louis David,* 1948.

M. Dommanget, *La déchristianisation à Beauvais et dans l'Oise,* 2 vols, 1918–22; *Sylvain Maréchal, 1750–1803,* 1950.

L. Madelin, *Fouché,* new edn, 1955.

L. Jacob, *Joseph Lebon,* 1932.

A. Soboul, "Sentiment religieux et cultes populaires", *A.h.R.F.,* 1957.

R. Cobb, "Les déduts de la déchristianisation à Dieppe", *A.h.R.F.,* 1956.

M. Reinhard et al., "Les prêtres abdicataires pendant la Révolution", *Actes du 89ᵉ Congrès des Sociétés Savantes,* Lyon 1964, pp. 27–228.

Index

Revised January, 1970

harper ⚜ torchbooks

American Studies: General

HENRY STEELE COMMAGER, Ed.: The Struggle for Racial Equality TB/1300

CARL N. DEGLER: Out of Our Past: *The Forces that Shaped Modern America* CN/2

CARL N. DEGLER, Ed.: Pivotal Interpretations of American History
Vol. I TB/1240; Vol. II TB/1241

A. S. EISENSTADT, Ed.: The Craft of American History: *Selected Essays*
Vol. I TB/1255; Vol. II TB/1256

ROBERT L. HEILBRONER: The Limits of American Capitalism TB/1305

JOHN HIGHAM, Ed.: The Reconstruction of American History TB/1068

ROBERT H. JACKSON: The Supreme Court in the American System of Government TB/1106

JOHN F. KENNEDY: A Nation of Immigrants. *Illus. Revised and Enlarged. Introduction by Robert F. Kennedy* TB/1118

RICHARD B. MORRIS: Fair Trial: *Fourteen Who Stood Accused, from Anne Hutchinson to Alger Hiss* TB/1335

GUNNAR MYRDAL: An American Dilemma: *The Negro Problem and Modern Democracy. Introduction by the Author.*
Vol. I TB/1443; Vol. II TB/1444

GILBERT OSOFSKY, Ed.: The Burden of Race: *A Documentary History of Negro-White Relations in America* TB/1405

ARNOLD ROSE: The Negro in America: *The Condensed Version of Gunnar Myrdal's* An American Dilemma. *Second Edition* TB/3048

JOHN E. SMITH: Themes in American Philosophy: *Purpose, Experience and Community* TB/1466

WILLIAM R. TAYLOR: Cavalier and Yankee: *The Old South and American National Character* TB/1474

American Studies: Colonial

BERNARD BAILYN: The New England Merchants in the Seventeenth Century TB/1149

ROBERT E. BROWN: Middle-Class Democracy and Revolution in Massachusetts, 1691–1780. *New Introduction by Author* TB/1413

JOSEPH CHARLES: The Origins of the American Party System TB/1049

WESLEY FRANK CRAVEN: The Colonies in Transition: 1660-1712† TB/3084

CHARLES GIBSON: Spain in America † TB/3077

CHARLES GIBSON, Ed.: The Spanish Tradition in America + HR/1351

LAWRENCE HENRY GIPSON: The Coming of the Revolution: 1763-1775. † *Illus.* TB/3007

PERRY MILLER: Errand Into the Wilderness TB/1139

PERRY MILLER & T. H. JOHNSON, Eds.: The Puritans: *A Sourcebook of Their Writings*
Vol. I TB/1093; Vol. II TB/1094

EDMUND S. MORGAN: The Puritan Family: *Religion and Domestic Relations in Seventeenth Century New England* TB/1227

WALLACE NOTESTEIN: The English People on the Eve of Colonization: 1603-1630. † *Illus.* TB/3006

LOUIS B. WRIGHT: The Cultural Life of the American Colonies: 1607-1763. † *Illus.* TB/3005

American Studies: The Revolution to 1860

JOHN R. ALDEN: The American Revolution: 1775-1783. † *Illus.* TB/3011

RAY A. BILLINGTON: The Far Western Frontier: 1830-1860. † *Illus.* TB/3012

GEORGE DANGERFIELD: The Awakening of American Nationalism, 1815-1828. † *Illus.* TB/3061

CLEMENT EATON: The Growth of Southern Civilization, 1790-1860. † *Illus.* TB/3040

LOUIS FILLER: The Crusade against Slavery: 1830-1860. † *Illus.* TB/3029

WILLIM W. FREEHLING: Prelude to Civil War: *The Nullification Controversy in South Carolina, 1816-1836* TB/1359

THOMAS JEFFERSON: Notes on the State of Virginia. ‡ *Edited by Thomas P. Abernethy* TB/3052

JOHN C. MILLER: The Federalist Era: 1789-1801. † *Illus.* TB/3027

RICHARD B. MORRIS: The American Revolution Reconsidered TB/1363

GILBERT OSOFSKY, Ed.: Puttin' On Ole Massa: *The Slave Narratives of Henry Bibb, William Wells Brown, and Solomon Northup* ‡ TB/1432

FRANCIS S. PHILBRICK: The Rise of the West, 1754-1830. † *Illus.* TB/3067

MARSHALL SMELSER: The Democratic Republic, 1801-1815 † TB/1406

† The New American Nation Series, edited by Henry Steele Commager and Richard B. Morris.
‡ American Perspectives series, edited by Bernard Wishy and William E. Leuchtenburg.
α History of Europe series, edited by J. H. Plumb.
§ The Library of Religion and Culture, edited by Benjamin Nelson.
‖ Researches in the Social, Cultural, and Behavioral Sciences, edited by Benjamin Nelson.
⅀ Harper Modern Science Series, edited by James A. Newman.
○ Not for sale in Canada.
+ Documentary History of the United States series, edited by Richard B. Morris.
# Documentary History of Western Civilization series, edited by Eugene C. Black and Leonard W. Levy.
∧ The Economic History of the United States series, edited by Henry David et al.
¶ European Perspectives series, edited by Eugene C. Black.
** Contemporary Essays series, edited by Leonard W. Levy.
* The Stratum Series, edited by John Hale.

1

LOUIS B. WRIGHT: Culture on the Moving Frontier TB/1053

American Studies: The Civil War to 1900

T. C. COCHRAN & WILLIAM MILLER: The Age of Enterprise: *A Social History of Industrial America* TB/1054
W. A. DUNNING: Reconstruction, Political and Economic: 1865-1877 TB/1073
HAROLD U. FAULKNER: Politics, Reform and Expansion: 1890-1900. † *Illus.* TB/3020
GEORGE M. FREDRICKSON: The Inner Civil War: *Northern Intellectuals and the Crisis of the Union* TB/1358
JOHN A. GARRATY: The New Commonwealth, 1877-1890 † TB/1410
HELEN HUNT JACKSON: A Century of Dishonor: *The Early Crusade for Indian Reform.* † *Edited by Andrew F. Rolle* TB/3063
WILLIAM G. MCLOUGHLIN, Ed.: The American Evangelicals, 1800-1900: An Anthology ‡ TB/1382
JAMES S. PIKE: The Prostrate State: *South Carolina under Negro Government.* ‡ *Intro. by Robert F. Durden* TB/3085
VERNON LANE WHARTON: The Negro in Mississippi, 1865-1890 TB/1178

American Studies: The Twentieth Century

RAY STANNARD BAKER: Following the Color Line: *American Negro Citizenship in Progressive Era.* ‡ *Edited by Dewey W. Grantham, Jr. Illus.* TB/3053
RANDOLPH S. BOURNE: War and the Intellectuals: *Collected Essays, 1915-1919.* ‡ *Edited by Carl Resek* TB/3043
A. RUSSELL BUCHANAN: The United States and World War II. † *Illus.*
Vol. I TB/3044; Vol. II TB/3045
THOMAS C. COCHRAN: The American Business System: *A Historical Perspective, 1900-1955* TB/1080
FOSTER RHEA DULLES: America's Rise to World Power: 1898-1954. † *Illus.* TB/3021
HAROLD U. FAULKNER: The Decline of Laissez Faire, 1897-1917 TB/1397
JOHN D. HICKS: Republican Ascendancy: 1921-1933. † *Illus.* TB/3041
WILLIAM E. LEUCHTENBURG: Franklin D. Roosevelt and the New Deal: 1932-1940. † *Illus.* TB/3025
WILLIAM E. LEUCHTENBURG, Ed.: The New Deal: *A Documentary History* † HR/1354
ARTHUR S. LINK: Woodrow Wilson and the Progressive Era: 1910-1917. † *Illus.* TB/3023
BROADUS MITCHELL: Depression Decade: *From New Era through New Deal, 1929-1941* ∆ TB/1439
GEORGE E. MOWRY: The Era of Theodore Roosevelt and the Birth of Modern America: 1900-1912. † *Illus.* TB/3022
WILLIAM PRESTON, JR.: Aliens and Dissenters:
TWELVE SOUTHERNERS: I'll Take My Stand: *The South and the Agrarian Tradition. Intro. by Louis D. Rubin, Jr.; Biographical Essays by Virginia Rock* TB/1072

Art, Art History, Aesthetics

ERWIN PANOFSKY: Renaissance and Renascences in Western Art. *Illus.* TB/1447
ERWIN PANOFSKY: Studies in Iconology: *Humanistic Themes in the Art of the Renaissance. 180 illus.* TB/1077
HEINRICH ZIMMER: Myths and Symbols in Indian Art and Civilization. *70 illus.* TB/2005

Asian Studies

WOLFGANG FRANKE: China and the West: *The Cultural Encounter, 13th to 20th Centuries. Trans. by R. A. Wilson* TB/1326
L. CARRINGTON GOODRICH: A Short History of the Chinese People. *Illus.* TB/3015

Economics & Economic History

C. E. BLACK: The Dynamics of Modernization: *A Study in Comparative History* TB/1321
GILBERT BURCK & EDITORS OF *Fortune:* The Computer Age: *And its Potential for Management* TB/1179
ROBERT L. HEILBRONER: The Future as History: *The Historic Currents of Our Time and the Direction in Which They Are Taking America* TB/1386
ROBERT L. HEILBRONER: The Great Ascent: *The Struggle for Economic Development in Our Time* TB/3030
FRANK H. KNIGHT: The Economic Organization TB/1214
DAVID S. LANDES: Bankers and Pashas: *International Finance and Economic Imperialism in Egypt. New Preface by the Author* TB/1412
ROBERT LATOUCHE: The Birth of Western Economy: *Economic Aspects of the Dark Ages* TB/1290
W. ARTHUR LEWIS: The Principles of Economic Planning. *New Introduction by the Author*° TB/1436
WILLIAM MILLER, Ed.: Men in Business: *Essays on the Historical Role of the Entrepreneur* TB/1081
HERBERT A. SIMON: The Shape of Automation: *For Men and Management* TB/1245

Historiography and History of Ideas

J. BRONOWSKI & BRUCE MAZLISH: The Western Intellectual Tradition: *From Leonardo to Hegel* TB/3001
WILHELM DILTHEY: Pattern and Meaning in History: *Thoughts on History and Society.*° *Edited with an Intro. by H. P. Rickman* TB/1075
J. H. HEXTER: More's Utopia: *The Biography of an Idea. Epilogue by the Author* TB/1195
H. STUART HUGHES: History as Art and as Science: *Twin Vistas on the Past* TB/1207
ARTHUR O. LOVEJOY: The Great Chain of Being: *A Study of the History of an Idea* TB/1009
RICHARD H. POPKIN: The History of Scepticism from Erasmus to Descartes. *Revised Edition* TB/1391
BRUNO SNELL: The Discovery of the Mind: *The Greek Origins of European Thought* TB/1018

History: General

HANS KOHN: The Age of Nationalism: *The First Era of Global History* TB/1380
BERNARD LEWIS: The Arabs in History TB/1029
BERNARD LEWIS: The Middle East and the West ° TB/1274

History: Ancient

A. ANDREWS: The Greek Tyrants TB/1103
THEODOR H. GASTER: Thespis: *Ritual Myth and Drama in the Ancient Near East* TB/1281

2

A. H. M. JONES, Ed.: A History of Rome through the Fifth Century # *Vol. I: The Republic* HR/1364
Vol. II The Empire: HR/1460
SAMUEL NOAH KRAMER: Sumerian Mythology TB/1055
NAPHTALI LEWIS & MEYER REINHOLD, Eds.: Roman Civilization *Vol. I: The Republic* TB/1231
Vol. II: The Empire TB/1232

History: Medieval

NORMAN COHN: The Pursuit of the Millennium: *Revolutionary Messianism in Medieval and Reformation Europe* TB/1037
F. L. GANSHOF: Feudalism TB/1058
F. L. GANSHOF: The Middle Ages: *A History of International Relations. Translated by Rémy Hall* TB/1411
HENRY CHARLES LEA: The Inquisition of the Middle Ages. || *Introduction by Walter Ullmann* TB/1456

History: Renaissance & Reformation

JACOB BURCKHARDT: The Civilization of the Renaissance in Italy. *Introduction by Benjamin Nelson and Charles Trinkaus. Illus.* Vol. I TB/40; Vol. II TB/41
JOHN CALVIN & JACOPO SADOLETO: A Reformation Debate. *Edited by John C. Olin* TB/1239
J. H. ELLIOTT: Europe Divided, 1559-1598 *a °* TB/1414
G. R. ELTON: Reformation Europe, 1517-1559 *° a* TB/1270
HANS J. HILLERBRAND, Ed., The Protestant Reformation # HR/1342
JOHAN HUIZINGA: Erasmus and the Age of Reformation. *Illus.* TB/19
JOEL HURSTFIELD: The Elizabethan Nation TB/1312
JOEL HURSTFIELD, Ed.: The Reformation Crisis TB/1267
PAUL OSKAR KRISTELLER: Renaissance Thought: *The Classic, Scholastic, and Humanist Strains* TB/1048
DAVID LITTLE: Religion, Order and Law: *A Study in Pre-Revolutionary England.* § *Preface by R. Bellah* TB/1418
PAOLO ROSSI: Philosophy, Technology, and the Arts, in the Early Modern Era 1400-1700. || *Edited by Benjamin Nelson. Translated by Salvator Attanasio* TB/1458
H. R. TREVOR-ROPER: The European Witch-craze of the Sixteenth and Seventeenth Centuries and Other Essays *°* TB/1416

History: Modern European

ALAN BULLOCK: Hitler, A Study in Tyranny. *° Revised Edition. Illus.* TB/1123
JOHANN GOTTLIEB FICHTE: Addresses to the German Nation. *Ed. with Intro. by George A. Kelly ¶* TB/1366
ALBERT GOODWIN: The French Revolution TB/1064
STANLEY HOFFMANN et al.: In Search of France: *The Economy, Society and Political System In the Twentieth Century* TB/1219
H. STUART HUGHES: The Obstructed Path: *French Social Thought in the Years of Desperation* TB/1451
JOHAN HUIZINGA: Dutch Civilisation in the 17th Century and Other Essays TB/1453

JOHN MCMANNERS: European History, 1789-1914: *Men, Machines and Freedom* TB/1419
HUGH SETON-WATSON: Eastern Europe Between the Wars, 1918-1941 TB/1330
ALBERT SOREL: Europe Under the Old Regime. *Translated by Francis H. Herrick* TB/1121
A. J. P. TAYLOR: From Napoleon to Lenin: *Historical Essays °* TB/1268
A. J. P. TAYLOR: The Habsburg Monarchy, 1809-1918: *A History of the Austrian Empire and Austria-Hungary °* TB/1187
J. M. THOMPSON: European History, 1494-1789 TB/1431
H. R. TREVOR-ROPER: Historical Essays TB/1269

Literature & Literary Criticism

W. J. BATE: From Classic to Romantic: *Premises of Taste in Eighteenth Century England* TB/1036
VAN WYCK BROOKS: Van Wyck Brooks: The Early Years: *A Selection from his Works, 1908-1921 Ed. with Intro. by Claire Sprague* TB/3082
RICHMOND LATTIMORE, Translator: The Odyssey of Homer TB/1389
ROBERT PREYER, Ed.: Victorian Literature ** TB/1302

Philosophy

HENRI BERGSON: Time and Free Will: *An Essay on the Immediate Data of Consciousness °* TB/1021
H. J. BLACKHAM: Six Existentialist Thinkers: *Kierkegaard, Nietzsche, Jaspers, Marcel, Heidegger, Sartre °* TB/1002
J. M. BOCHENSKI: The Methods of Contemporary Thought. *Trans. by Peter Caws* TB/1377
ERNST CASSIRER: Rousseau, Kant and Goethe. *Intro. by Peter Gay* TB/1092
MICHAEL GELVEN: A Commentary on Heidegger's "Being and Time" TB/1464
J. GLENN GRAY: Hegel and Greek Thought TB/1409
W. K. C. GUTHRIE: The Greek Philosophers: *From Thales to Aristotle °* TB/1008
G. W. F. HEGEL: Phenomenology of Mind. *° || Introduction by George Lichtheim* TB/1303
MARTIN HEIDEGGER: Discourse on Thinking. *Translated with a Preface by John M. Anderson and E. Hans Freund. Introduction by John M. Anderson* TB/1459
F. H. HEINEMANN: Existentialism and the Modern Predicament TB/28
WERER HEISENBERG: Physics and Philosophy: *The Revolution in Modern Science. Intro. by F. S. C. Northrop* TB/549
EDMUND HUSSERL: Phenomenology and the Crisis of Philosophy. § *Translated with an Introduction by Quentin Lauer* TB/1170
IMMANUEL KANT: Groundwork of the Metaphysic of Morals. *Translated and Analyzed by H. J. Paton* TB/1159
WALTER KAUFMANN, Ed.: Religion From Tolstoy to Camus: *Basic Writings on Religious Truth and Morals* TB/123
QUENTIN LAUER: Phenomenology: *Its Genesis and Prospect. Preface by Aron Gurwitsch* TB/1169
MICHAEL POLANYI: Personal Knowledge: *Towards a Post-Critical Philosophy* TB/1158
WILLARD VAN ORMAN QUINE: Elementary Logic *Revised Edition* TB/577
WILHELM WINDELBAND: A History of Philosophy *Vol. I: Greek, Roman, Medieval* TB/38

3

Vol. II: Renaissance, Enlightenment, Modern
TB/39
LUDWIG WITTGENSTEIN: The Blue and Brown Books °   TB/1211
LUDWIG WITTGENSTEIN: Notebooks, 1914-1916
TB/1441

Political Science & Government

C. E. BLACK: The Dynamics of Modernization: *A Study in Comparative History*   TB/1321
DENIS W. BROGAN: Politics in America. *New Introduction by the Author*   TB/1469
ROBERT CONQUEST: Power and Policy in the USSR: *The Study of Soviet Dynastics* °
TB/1307
JOHN B. MORRALL: Political Thought in Medieval Times   TB/1076
KARL R. POPPER: The Open Society and Its Enemies *Vol. I: The Spell of Plato*   TB/1101
Vol. II: The High Tide of Prophecy: Hegel, Marx, and the Aftermath   TB/1102
HENRI DE SAINT-SIMON: Social Organization, The Science of Man, and Other Writings. || *Edited and Translated with an Introduction by Felix Markham*   TB/1152
CHARLES SCHOTTLAND, Ed.: The Welfare State **
TB/1323
JOSEPH A. SCHUMPETER: Capitalism, Socialism and Democracy   TB/3008

Psychology

LUDWIG BINSWANGER: Being-in-the-World: *Selected Papers. || Trans. with Intro. by Jacob Needleman*   TB/1365
MIRCEA ELIADE: Cosmos and History: *The Myth of the Eternal Return* §   TB/2050
MIRCEA ELIADE: Myth and Reality   TB/1369
SIGMUND FREUD: On Creativity and the Unconscious: *Papers on the Psychology of Art, Literature, Love, Religion.* § *Intro. by Benjamin Nelson*   TB/45
J. GLENN GRAY: The Warriors: *Reflections on Men in Battle. Introduction by Hannah Arendt*   TB/1294
WILLIAM JAMES: Psychology: *The Briefer Course. Edited with an Intro. by Gordon Allport*   TB/1034

Religion: Ancient and Classical, Biblical and Judaic Traditions

MARTIN BUBER: Eclipse of God: *Studies in the Relation Between Religion and Philosophy*
TB/12
MARTIN BUBER: Hasidism and Modern Man. *Edited and Translated by Maurice Friedman*
TB/839
MARTIN BUBER: The Knowledge of Man. *Edited with an Introduction by Maurice Friedman. Translated by Maurice Friedman and Ronald Gregor Smith*   TB/135
MARTIN BUBER: Moses. *The Revelation and the Covenant*   TB/837
MARTIN BUBER: The Origin and Meaning of Hasidism. *Edited and Translated by Maurice Friedman*   TB/835
MARTIN BUBER: The Prophetic Faith   TB/73
MARTIN BUBER: Two Types of Faith: *Interpenetration of Judaism and Christianity* °   TB/75
M. S. ENSLIN: Christian Beginnings   TB/5
M. S. ENSLIN: The Literature of the Christian Movement   TB/6
HENRI FRANKFORT: Ancient Egyptian Religion: *An Interpretation*   TB/77

Religion: Early Christianity Through Reformation

ANSELM OF CANTERBURY: Truth, Freedom, and Evil: *Three Philosophical Dialogues. Edited and Translated by Jasper Hopkins and Herbert Richardson*   TB/317
EDGAR J. GOODSPEED: A Life of Jesus   TB/1
ROBERT M. GRANT: Gnosticism and Early Christianity   TB/136

Religion: Oriental Religions

TOR ANDRAE: Mohammed: *The Man and His Faith* §   TB/62
EDWARD CONZE: Buddhism: *Its Essence and Development.* ° *Foreword by Arthur Waley*
TB/58
H. G. CREEL: Confucius and the Chinese Way
TB/63
FRANKLIN EDGERTON, Trans. & Ed.: The Bhagavad Gita   TB/115
SWAMI NIKHILANANDA, Trans. & Ed.: The Upanishads   TB/114
D. T. SUZUKI: On Indian Mahayana Buddhism. ° *Ed. with Intro. by Edward Conze.* TB/1403

Science and Mathematics

W. E. LE GROS CLARK: The Antecedents of Man: *An Introduction to the Evolution of the Primates.* ° *Illus.*   TB/559
ROBERT E. COKER: Streams, Lakes, Ponds. *Illus.*
TB/586
ROBERT E. COKER: This Great and Wide Sea: *An Introduction to Oceanography and Marine Biology. Illus.*   TB/551
WILLARD VAN ORMAN QUINE: Mathematical Logic
TB/558

Sociology and Anthropology

REINHARD BENDIX: Work and Authority in Industry: *Ideologies of Management in the Course of Industrialization*   TB/3035
KENNETH B. CLARK: Dark Ghetto: *Dilemmas of Social Power. Foreword by Gunnar Myrdal*
TB/1317
KENNETH CLARK & JEANNETTE HOPKINS: A Relevant War Against Poverty: *A Study of Community Action Programs and Observable Social Change*   TB/1480
LEWIS COSER, Ed.: Political Sociology   TB/1293
GARY T. MARX: Protest and Prejudice: *A Study of Belief in the Black Community*   TB/1435
ROBERT K. MERTON, LEONARD BROOM, LEONARD S. COTTRELL, JR., Editors: Sociology Today: *Problems and Prospects* ||
Vol. I TB/1173; Vol. II TB/1174
GILBERT OSOFSKY, Ed.: The Burden of Race: A Documentary History of Negro-White Relations in America   TB/1405
GILBERT OSOFSKY: Harlem: The Making of a Ghetto: *Negro New York 1890-1930* °   TB/1381
PHILIP RIEFF: The Triumph of the Therapeutic: *Uses of Faith After Freud*   TB/1360
ARNOLD ROSE: The Negro in America: *The Condensed Version of Gunnar Myrdal's An American Dilemma. Second Edition*   TB/3048
GEORGE ROSEN: Madness in Society: *Chapters in the Historical Sociology of Mental Illness. || Preface by Benjamin Nelson*   TB/1337
PITIRIM A. SOROKIN: Contemporary Sociological Theories: *Through the First Quarter of the Twentieth Century*   TB/3046
FLORIAN ZNANIECKI: The Social Role of the Man of Knowledge. *Introduction by Lewis A. Coser*   TB/1372